Monitoring Docker

Monitor your Docker containers and their apps using various native and third-party tools with the help of this exclusive guide!

Russ McKendrick

[PACKT] open source
PUBLISHING
community experience distilled

BIRMINGHAM - MUMBAI

Monitoring Docker

First published: December 2015

Production reference: 1041215

Published by Packt Publishing Ltd.
Livery Place
35 Livery Street
Birmingham B3 2PB, UK.

ISBN 978-1-78588-275-3

www.packtpub.com

Credits

Author
Russ McKendrick

Reviewer
Marcelo Correia Pinheiro

Commissioning Editor
Veena Pagare

Acquisition Editor
Rahul Nair

Content Development Editor
Anish Sukumaran

Technical Editor
Saurabh Malhotra

Copy Editor
Trishya Hajare

Project Coordinator
Izzat Contractor

Proofreader
Safis Editing

Indexers
Mariammal Chettiyar

Priya Sane

Production Coordinator
Shantanu N. Zagade

Cover Work
Shantanu N. Zagade

About the Author

Russ McKendrick is an experienced solutions architect who has been working in IT and IT-related industries for the better part of 23 years. During his career, he has had varied responsibilities in a number of industries, ranging from looking after entire IT infrastructures to providing first line, second line, and senior support in client facing, and internal teams for corporate organizations.

He works almost exclusively with Linux, using open source systems and tools on various platforms ranging from dedicated hardware and virtual machines to public clouds.

About the Reviewer

Marcelo Correia Pinheiro is a Brazilian software engineer from Porto Alegre. He started to work as a web designer and programmer in 2000 with ASP and PHP, naturally getting in touch with the Microsoft .NET framework and Java running respective databases of choice for web applications. Since 2003, he has used Linux and UNIX-related operational systems, from Slackware to Gobo Linux, Archlinux, CentOS, Debian, and today OSX, having some contact with BSD distributions too. He has lost some nights compiling and applying patches to the Linux kernel to make its desktop work. Since the beginning, he has been acting as a problem solver, no matter what the programming language, database, or platform is — open source enthusiast.

After a few years, he decided to live in São Paulo to work with newer technologies such as NoSQL, cloud computing, and Ruby, where he started to conduct tech talks with this language in Locaweb. He created some tools to standardize development using tools such as vagrant and Ruby gems — some of these in their GitHub — in Locaweb to ensure fast application packaging and reduced deployment rollbacks. In 2013, he changed his career to be a full-stack developer following the DevOps movement. Since 2012, he has attended, as a speaker, some of the biggest software conferences in Brazil — RS on Rails, QConSP, The Developer's Conference, and RubyConf Brazil — talking not only about Ruby, but also about some of the well-known DevOps tools such as Terraform, Packer, Ansible, and Docker. Today, he works as a DevOps consultant in their company.

In his free time, he loves playing the guitar, having some fun with cats, traveling, and drinking beer. He can be found on his blog (`http://salizzar.net`), Twitter (`https://twitter.com/salizzar`), GitHub (`https://github.com/salizzar`) and Linkedin (`https://www.linkedin.com/in/salizzar`).

He has worked as a reviewer for *Vagrant Virtual Development Environment Cookbook*, a Packt Publishing book with useful recipes using vagrant with configuration management tools such as Puppet, Chef, Ansible, and SaltStack.

I want to thank all my friends, who believed in my potential since the beginning and who still follow me despite the distance. I would also like to thank my mentors, Gleicon Moraes, Roberto Gaiser, and Rodrigo Campos, who gave me the incentive and tips to be a better software engineer and person.

www.PacktPub.com

Support files, eBooks, discount offers, and more

For support files and downloads related to your book, please visit www.PacktPub.com.

Did you know that Packt offers eBook versions of every book published, with PDF and ePub files available? You can upgrade to the eBook version at www.PacktPub.com and as a print book customer, you are entitled to a discount on the eBook copy. Get in touch with us at service@packtpub.com for more details.

At www.PacktPub.com, you can also read a collection of free technical articles, sign up for a range of free newsletters and receive exclusive discounts and offers on Packt books and eBooks.

https://www2.packtpub.com/books/subscription/packtlib

Do you need instant solutions to your IT questions? PacktLib is Packt's online digital book library. Here, you can search, access, and read Packt's entire library of books.

Why subscribe?

- Fully searchable across every book published by Packt
- Copy and paste, print, and bookmark content
- On demand and accessible via a web browser

Free access for Packt account holders

If you have an account with Packt at www.PacktPub.com, you can use this to access PacktLib today and view 9 entirely free books. Simply use your login credentials for immediate access.

Table of Contents

Preface

With the increase in the adoption of Docker containers, the need to monitor which containers are running, what resources they are consuming, and how it affects the overall performance of the system, has become a time-related need. *Monitoring Docker* will teach you how monitoring containers and keeping a keen eye on the working of applications help to improve the overall performance of the applications that run on Docker.

This book will cover monitoring containers using Docker's native monitoring functions, various plugins, and also third-party tools that help in monitoring. The book will first cover how to obtain detailed stats for the active containers, resources consumed, and container behavior. This book will also show the readers how to use these stats to improve the overall performance of the system.

What this book covers

Chapter 1, *Introduction to Docker Monitoring*, discusses how different it is to monitor containers compared to more traditional servers such as virtual machines, bare metal machines, and cloud instances (Pets versus Cattle and Chickens versus Snowflakes). This chapter also details the operating systems covered in the examples later in this book and also gives a little information on how to get a local test environment up and running using vagrant, so that installation instructions and practical examples can be easily followed.

Chapter 2, *Using the Built-in Tools*, helps you learn about the basic metrics you can get out of the vanilla Docker installation and how you can use them. Also, we will understand how to get real-time statistics on our running containers, how to use commands that are familiar to us, and how to get information on the processes that are launched as part of each container.

Chapter 3, *Advanced Container Resource Analysis*, introduces cAdvisor from Google, which adds a lot more precision to the basic tools provided by Docker. You will also learn how to install cAdvisor and start collecting metrics.

Chapter 4, *A Traditional Approach to Monitoring Containers*, looks at a traditional tool for monitoring services. By the end of this chapter, you should know your way around Zabbix and the various ways you can monitor your containers.

Chapter 5, *Querying with Sysdig*, describes Sysdig as "an open source, system-level exploration tool to capture system state and activity from a running Linux instance, then save, filter, and analyze it." In this chapter, you will learn how to use Sysdig to both view your containers' performance metrics in real time and also record sessions to query later.

Chapter 6, *Exploring Third Party Options*, walks you through a few of the Software as a Service (SaaS) options that are available, why you would use them, and how to install their clients on the host server.

Chapter 7, *Collecting Application Logs from within the Container*, looks at how we can get the content of the log files for the applications running within our containers to a central location so that they are available even if you have to destroy and replace a container.

Chapter 8, *What Are the Next Steps?*, looks at the next steps you can take in monitoring your containers by talking about the benefits of adding alerting to your monitoring. Also, we will cover some different scenarios and look at which type of monitoring is appropriate for each of them.

What you need for this book

To ensure the experience is as consistent as possible, we will be installing vagrant and VirtualBox to run the virtual machine that will act as a host to run our containers. Vagrant is available for Linux, OS X, and Windows; for details on how to install this, see the vagrant website at `https://www.vagrantup.com/`. The details of how to download and install VirtualBox can be found at `https://www.virtualbox.org/`; again, VirtualBox can be installed on Linux, OS X, and Windows.

Who this book is for

This book is for DevOps engineers and system administrators who want to manage Docker containers, better manage these containers using expert techniques and methods, and better maintain applications built on Docker.

Conventions

In this book, you will find a number of text styles that distinguish between different kinds of information. Here are some examples of these styles and an explanation of their meaning.

Code words in text, database table names, folder names, filenames, file extensions, pathnames, dummy URLs, user input, and Twitter handles are shown as follows: "We can include other contexts through the use of the `include` directive."

A block of code is set as follows:

```
{
  "fields": {
    "@timestamp": [
      1444567706641
    ]
  },
  "sort": [
    1444567706641
  ]
}
```

When we wish to draw your attention to a particular part of a code block, the relevant lines or items are set in bold:

```
{
  "fields": {
    "@timestamp": [
      1444567706641
    ]
  },
  "sort": [
    1444567706641
  ]
}
```

Any command-line input or output is written as follows:

```
cd ~/Documents/Projects/monitoring-docker/vagrant-ubuntu
vagrant up
```

New terms and **important words** are shown in bold. Words that you see on the screen, for example, in menus or dialog boxes, appear in the text like this: "Clicking the **Next** button moves you to the next screen."

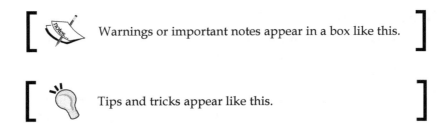

Warnings or important notes appear in a box like this.

Tips and tricks appear like this.

Reader feedback

Feedback from our readers is always welcome. Let us know what you think about this book—what you liked or disliked. Reader feedback is important for us as it helps us develop titles that you will really get the most out of.

To send us general feedback, simply e-mail feedback@packtpub.com, and mention the book's title in the subject of your message.

If there is a topic that you have expertise in and you are interested in either writing or contributing to a book, see our author guide at www.packtpub.com/authors.

Customer support

Now that you are the proud owner of a Packt book, we have a number of things to help you to get the most from your purchase.

Downloading the example code

You can download the example code files from your account at http://www.packtpub.com for all the Packt Publishing books you have purchased. If you purchased this book elsewhere, you can visit http://www.packtpub.com/support and register to have the files e-mailed directly to you.

Downloading the color images of this book

We also provide you with a PDF file that has color images of the screenshots/diagrams used in this book. The color images will help you better understand the changes in the output. You can download this file from: http://www.packtpub.com/sites/default/files/downloads/Monitoring_Docker_ColorImages.pdf.

Errata

Although we have taken every care to ensure the accuracy of our content, mistakes do happen. If you find a mistake in one of our books—maybe a mistake in the text or the code—we would be grateful if you could report this to us. By doing so, you can save other readers from frustration and help us improve subsequent versions of this book. If you find any errata, please report them by visiting `http://www.packtpub.com/submit-errata`, selecting your book, clicking on the **Errata Submission Form** link, and entering the details of your errata. Once your errata are verified, your submission will be accepted and the errata will be uploaded to our website or added to any list of existing errata under the Errata section of that title.

To view the previously submitted errata, go to `https://www.packtpub.com/books/content/support` and enter the name of the book in the search field. The required information will appear under the **Errata** section.

Piracy

Piracy of copyrighted material on the Internet is an ongoing problem across all media. At Packt, we take the protection of our copyright and licenses very seriously. If you come across any illegal copies of our works in any form on the Internet, please provide us with the location address or website name immediately so that we can pursue a remedy.

Please contact us at `copyright@packtpub.com` with a link to the suspected pirated material.

We appreciate your help in protecting our authors and our ability to bring you valuable content.

Questions

If you have a problem with any aspect of this book, you can contact us at `questions@packtpub.com`, and we will do our best to address the problem.

1
Introduction to Docker Monitoring

Docker has been a recent but very important addition to a SysAdmins toolbox.

Docker describes itself as an open platform for building, shipping, and running distributed applications. This means that developers can bundle their code and pass it to their operations team. From here, they can deploy safe in the knowledge that it will be done so in a way that introduces consistency with the environment in which the code is running.

When this process is followed, it should make the age-old developers versus operations argument of "it worked on my local development server" — a thing of the past. Since before its "production ready" 1.0 release back in June 2014, there had been over 10,000 Dockerized applications available. By the end of 2014, that number had risen to over 71,000. You can see how Docker grew in 2014 by looking at the infographic that was published by Docker in early 2015, which can be found at https://blog.docker.com/2015/01/docker-project-2014-a-whirlwind-year-in-review/.

While the debate is still raging about how production ready the technology is, Docker has gained an impressive list of technology partners, including RedHat, Canonical, HP, and even Microsoft.

Companies such as Google, Spotify, Soundcloud, and CenturyLink, have all open sourced tools that support Docker in some way, shape, or form and there has also been numerous independent developers who have released apps that provide additional functionality to the core Docker product set. Also, all the companies have sprung up around the Docker ecosystem.

This book assumes that you have had some level of experience building, running, and managing Docker containers, and that you would now like to start to metrics from your running applications to further tune them, or that you would like to know when a problem occurs with a container so that you can debug any ongoing issues.

If you have never used Docker before, you may want to try one of the excellent books that serve and introduce you to all the things that Docker provides, books such as *Learning Docker, Packt Publishing*, or Docker's own introduction to containers, which can be found at their documentation pages, as follows:

- Learning Docker: `https://www.packtpub.com/virtualization-and-cloud/learning-docker`
- Official Docker docs: `https://docs.docker.com/`

Now, we have a brought ourselves up to speed with what Docker is; the rest of this chapter will cover the following topics:

- How different is it to monitor containers versus more traditional servers such as virtual machines, bare metal machine, and cloud instances (Pets, Cattle, Chickens, and Snowflakes).
- What are the minimum versions of Docker you should be running?
- How to follow instructions on bringing up an environment locally using Vagrant in order to follow the practical exercises in this book

Pets, Cattle, Chickens, and Snowflakes

Before we start discussing the various ways in which you can monitor your containers, we should get an understanding of what a SysAdmins world looks like these days and also where containers fit into it.

A typical SysAdmin will probably be looking after an estate of servers that are hosted in either an on-site or third-party data center, some may even manage instances hosted in a public cloud such as Amazon Web Services or Microsoft Azure, and some SysAdmins may juggle all their server estates across multiple hosting environments.

Each of these different environments has its own way of doing things, as well as performing best practices. Back in February 2012, Randy Bias gave a talk at Cloudscaling that discussed architectures for open and scalable clouds. Towards the end of the slide deck, Randy introduced the concept of Pets versus Cattle (which he attributes to Bill Baker, who was then an engineer at Microsoft).

You can view the original slide deck at http://www.slideshare.net/randybias/architecture-for-open-and-scalable-clouds.

Pets versus Cattle is now widely accepted as a good analogy to describe modern hosting practices.

Pets

Pets are akin to traditional physical servers or virtual machines, as follows:

- Each pet has a name; for example, myserver.domain.com.

- When they're not well, you take them to the vet to help them get better. You employ SysAdmins to look after them.

- You pay close attention to them, sometimes for years. You take backups, patch them, and ensure that they are fully documented.

Cattle

Cattle, on the other hand, represent more modern cloud computing instances, as follows:

- You've got too many to name, so you give them numbers; for example, the URL could look something like ip123123123123.eu.public-cloud.com.

- When they get sick, you shoot them and if your herd requires it, you replace anything you've killed: A server crashes or shows signs that it is having problems, you terminate it and your configuration automatically replaces it with an exact replica.

- You put them in a field and watch them from far and you don't expect them to live long. Rather than monitoring the individual instances, you monitor the cluster. When more resources are needed, you add more instances and once the resource is no longer required, you terminate the instances to get you back to your base configuration.

Chickens

Next up is a term that is a good way of describing how containers fit into the Pets versus Cattle world; in a blog post title "Cloud Computing: Pets, Cattle and ... Chickens?" on ActiveState, Bernard Golden describes containers as Chickens:

- They're more efficient than cattle when it comes to resource use. A container can boot in seconds where a instance or server can take minutes; it also uses less CPU power than a typical virtual machine or cloud instance.

- There are many more chickens than cattle. You can quite densely pack containers onto your instances or servers.

- Chickens tend to have a shorter lifespan than cattle and pets. Containers lend themselves to running micros-services; these containers may only be active for a few minutes.

The original blog post can be found at `http://www.activestate.com/blog/2015/02/cloud-computing-pets-cattle-and-chickens`.

Snowflakes

The final term is not animal-related and it describes a type of server that you defiantly don't want to have in your server estate, a Snowflake. This term was penned by Martin Fowler in a blog post titled "SnowflakeServer". Snowflakes is a term applied to "legacy" or "inherited" servers:

- Snowflakes are delicate and are treated with kid gloves. Typically, the server has been in the data center since you started. No one knows who originally configured it and there is no documentation of it; all you know is that it is important.

- Each one is unique and is impossible to exactly reproduce. Even the most hardened SysAdmin fears to reboot the machine incase it doesn't boot afterwards, as it is running end-of-life software that can not easily be reinstalled.

Martin's post can be found at `http://martinfowler.com/bliki/SnowflakeServer.html`.

So what does this all mean?

Depending on your requirements and the application you want to deploy, your containers can be launched onto either pet or cattle style servers. You can also create a clutch of chickens and have your containers run micro-services.

Also, in theory, you can replace your feared snowflake servers with a container-based application that meets all the end-of-life software requirements while remaining deployable on a modern supportable platform.

Each of the different styles of server has different monitoring requirements, in the final chapter we will look at Pets, Cattle, Chickens, and Snowflakes again and discuss the tools we have covered in the coming chapters. We will also cover best practices you should take into consideration when planning your monitoring.

Docker

While Docker hit its version 1.0 milestone over a year ago, it is still in it's infancy; with each new release comes new features, bug fixes, and even support for some early functionality that is being depreciated.

Docker itself is now a collection of several smaller projects; these include the following:

- Docker Engine
- Docker Machine
- Docker Compose
- Docker Swarm
- Docker Hub
- Docker Registry
- Kitmatic

In this book, we will be using Docker Engine, Docker Compose, and the Docker Hub.

Docker Engine is the core component of the Docker project and it provides the main bulk of the Docker functionality. Whenever Docker or the `docker` command is mentioned in this book, I will be referring to Docker Engine.

The book assumes you have Docker Engine version 1.71 or later installed; older versions of Docker Engine may not contain the necessary functionality required to run the commands and software covered in the upcoming chapters.

Docker Compose started its life as a third-party orchestration tool called **Fig** before being purchased by Docker in 2014. It is described as a way of defining a multi-container application using YAML (`http://yaml.org`). Simply put, this means that you quickly deploy complex applications using a single command that calls a human readable configuration file.

We assume that you have Docker Compose 1.3.3 or later installed; the `docker-compose.yml` files mentioned in this book have been written with this version in mind.

Finally, the majority of the images we will be deploying during this book will be sourced from the Docker Hub (`https://hub.docker.com/`), which not only houses a public registry containing over 40,000 public images but also 100 official images. The following screenshot shows the official repositories listing on the Docker Hub website:

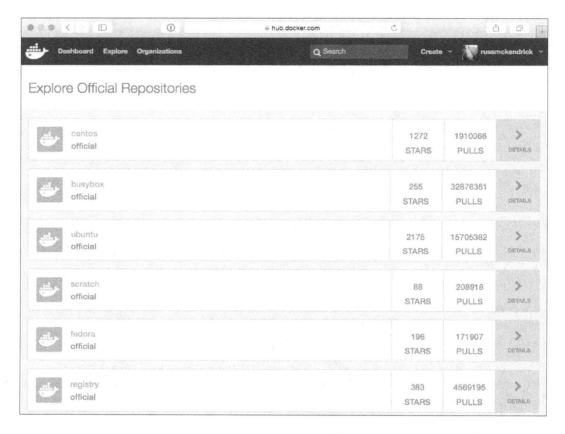

You can also sign up and use the Docker Hub to host your own public and private images.

Launching a local environment

Wherever possible, I will try to ensure that the practical exercises in this book will be able to be run on a local machine such as your desktop or laptop. For the purposes of this book, I will assume that your local machine is running either a recent version OS X or an up-to-date Linux distribution and has a high enough specification to run the software mentioned in this chapter.

The two tools we will be using to launch our Docker instances will also run on Windows; therefore, it should be possible to follow the instructions within this, although you may have to refer the usage guides for any changes to the syntax.

Due to the way in which Docker is architected, a lot of the content of this book will have you running commands and interacting with the command line on the virtual server that is acting as the host machine, rather than the containers themselves. Because of this, we will not be using either Docker Machine or Kitematic.

Both of these are tools provided by Docker to quickly bootstrap a Docker-enabled virtual server on your local machine, as unfortunately the host machines deployed by these tools contain a stripped down operating system that is optimized for running Docker with the smallest footprint as possible.

As we will be installing additional packages on the host machines, a stripped down "Docker only" operating system may not have the components available to meet the prerequisites of the software that we will be running in the later chapters; therefore, to ensure that there are no problems further on, we be running a full operating system.

Personally, I prefer a RPM-based operating system such as RedHat Enterprise Linux, Fedora, or CentOS, as I have been using them pretty much since the day I first logged into a Linux server.

However, as a lot of readers will be familiar with the Debian-based Ubuntu, I will be providing practical examples for both operating systems.

To ensure the experience is as consistent as possible, we will be installing Vagrant and VirtualBox to run the virtual machine that will act as a host to run our containers.

Vagrant, written by Mitchell Hashimoto, is a command line tool for creating and configuring reproducible and portable virtual machine environments. There have been numerous blog posts and articles that actually pitch Docker against Vagrant; however, in our case, the two technologies work quite well together in providing a repeatable and consistent environment.

Vagrant is available for Linux, OS X, and Windows. For details on how to install, go to the Vagrant website at `https://www.vagrantup.com/`.

VirtualBox is a great all round open source virtualization platform originally developed by Sun and now maintained by Oracle. It allows you to run both 32-bit and 64-bit guest operating systems on your local machine. Details on how to download and install VirtualBox can be found at `https://www.virtualbox.org/`; again, VirtualBox can be installed on Linux, OS X, and Windows.

Cloning the environment

The source for the environment along with the practical examples can be found on GitHub in the Monitoring Docker repository at https://github.com/russmckendrick/monitoring-docker.

To clone the repository on a terminal on your local machine, run the following commands (replacing the file path as needed):

```
mkdir ~/Documents/Projects
cd ~/Documents/Projects/
git clone https://github.com/russmckendrick/monitoring-docker.git
```

Once cloned, you should see a directory called `monitoring-docker` and then enter that directory, as follows:

```
cd ~/Documents/Projects/monitoring-docker
```

Running a virtual server

In the repository, you will find two folders containing the necessary `Vagrant` file to launch either a CentOS 7 or a Ubuntu 14.04 virtual server.

If you would like to use the CentOS 7 vagrant box, change the directory to `vagrant-centos`:

```
cd vagrant-centos
```

Once you are in the vagrant-centos directory, you will see that there is a `Vagrant` file; this file is all you need to launch a CentOS 7 virtual server. After the virtual server has been booted, the latest version of `docker` and `docker-compose` will be installed and the `monitoring-docker` directory will also be mounted inside the virtual machine using the mount point `/monitoring-docker`.

To launch the virtual server, simply type the following command:

```
vagrant up
```

This will download the latest version of the vagrant box from https://atlas.hashicorp.com/russmckendrick/boxes/centos71 and then boot the virtual server; it's a 450 MB download so it may take several minutes to download; it only has to do this once.

If all goes well, you should see something similar to the following output:

Now that you have booted the virtual server, you can connect to it using the following command:

```
vagrant ssh
```

Once logged in, you should verify that docker and docker-compose are both available:

Finally, you can try running the hello-world container using the following command:

```
docker run hello-world
```

If everything goes as expected, you should see the following output:

To try something more ambitious, you can run an Ubuntu container with the following command:

```
docker run -it ubuntu bash
```

Before we launch and enter the Ubuntu container, lets confirm that we are running the CentOS host machine by checking the release file that can be found in /etc:

Now, we can launch the Ubuntu container. Using the same command, we can confirm that we are inside the Ubuntu container by viewing its release file:

```
[vagrant@docker ~]$ docker run -it ubuntu bash
Unable to find image 'ubuntu:latest' locally
latest: Pulling from library/ubuntu

c63fb41c2213: Pull complete
99fcaefe76ef: Pull complete
5a4526e952f0: Pull complete
1d073211c498: Pull complete
Digest: sha256:8b1bffa54d8a58395bae61ec32f1a70fc82a939e4a7179e6277eb79e4c3c56f6
Status: Downloaded newer image for ubuntu:latest
root@dc806c481067:/# cat /etc/*release
DISTRIB_ID=Ubuntu
DISTRIB_RELEASE=14.04
DISTRIB_CODENAME=trusty
DISTRIB_DESCRIPTION="Ubuntu 14.04.3 LTS"
NAME="Ubuntu"
VERSION="14.04.3 LTS, Trusty Tahr"
ID=ubuntu
ID_LIKE=debian
PRETTY_NAME="Ubuntu 14.04.3 LTS"
VERSION_ID="14.04"
HOME_URL="http://www.ubuntu.com/"
SUPPORT_URL="http://help.ubuntu.com/"
BUG_REPORT_URL="http://bugs.launchpad.net/ubuntu/"
root@dc806c481067:/# []
```

To exit the container just type in `exit`. This will stop the container from running, as it has terminated the only running process within the container, which was bash, and returned you to the host CentOS machine.

As you can see here from our CentOS 7 host, we have launched and removed an Ubuntu container.

Both the CentOS 7 and Ubuntu Vagrant files will configure a static IP address on your virtual machine. It is `192.168.33.10`; also, there is a DNS record for this IP address available at `docker.media-glass.es`. These will allow you to access any containers that expose themselves to a browser at either `http://192.168.33.10/` or `http://docker.media-glass.es/`.

The URL `http://docker.media-glass.es/` will only work while the vagrant box is up, and you have a container running which serves Web pages.

You can see this in action by running the following command:

```
docker run -d -p 80:80russmckendrick/nginx-php
```

Downloading the example code

You can download the example code files from your account at `http://www.packtpub.com` for all the Packt Publishing books you have purchased. If you purchased this book elsewhere, you can visit `http://www.packtpub.com/support` and register to have the files e-mailed directly to you.

This will download and launch a container running NGINX. You can then go to `http://192.168.33.10/` or `http://docker.media-glass.es/` in your browser; you should see a forbidden page. This is because we have not yet given NGINX any content to serve (more on this will be covered later in the book):

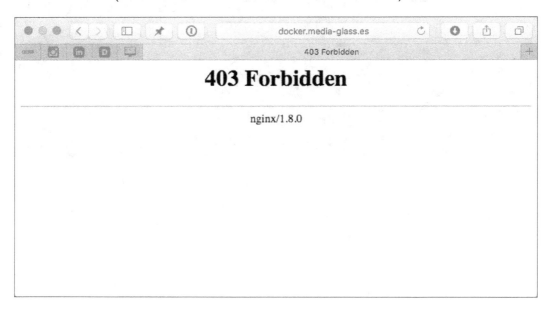

For more examples and ideas, go to the website at `http://docs.docker.com/userguide/`.

Halting the virtual server

To log out of the virtual server and return to your local machine, you type `exit`.

You should now see your local machine's terminal prompt; however, the virtual server you booted will still be running in the background happily, using resources, until you either power it down using the following command:

`vagrant halt`

Terminate the virtual server altogether using `vagrant destroy`:

`vagrant destroy`

To check the current status of the virtual server, you can run the following command:

`vagrant status`

The result of the preceding command is given in the following output:

Either powering the virtual server back on or creating it from scratch again, can be achieved by issuing the vagrant up command again.

The preceding details show how to use the CentOS 7 vagrant box. If you would prefer to launch an Ubuntu 14.04 virtual server, you can download and install the vagrant box by going into the vagrant-ubuntu directory using the following command:

`cd ~/Documents/Projects/monitoring-docker/vagrant-ubuntu`

`vagrant up`

From here, you will be able run vagrant up and follow the same instructions used to boot and interact with the CentOS 7 virtual server.

Summary

In this chapter, we talked about different types of server and also discussed how your containerized applications can fit into each of the categories. We have also installed VirtualBox and used Vagrant to launch either a CentOS 7 or Ubuntu 14.04 virtual server, with docker and docker-compose installed.

Our new virtual server environment will be used throughout the upcoming chapters to test the various different types of monitoring. In the next chapter, we will start our journey by using Docker's in-built functionality to explore metrics about our running containers.

2
Using the Built-in Tools

In the later chapters of this book, we will explore the monitoring parts of the large eco-system that has started to flourish around Docker over the last 24 months. However, before we press ahead with that, we should take a look at what is possible with a vanilla installation of Docker. In this chapter, we will cover the following topics:

- Using the tools built into Docker to get real-time metrics on container performance
- Using standard operating system commands to get metrics on what Docker is doing
- Generating a test load so you can view the metrics changing

Docker stats

Since version 1.5, there has been a basic statistic command built into Docker:

```
docker stats --help


Usage: docker stats [OPTIONS] CONTAINER [CONTAINER...]


Display a live stream of one or more containers' resource usage
statistics


  --help=false          Print usage
  --no-stream=false     Disable streaming stats and only pull the first
result
```

This command will stream details of the resource utilization of your containers in real time. The best way to find out about the command is to see it in action.

Running Docker stats

Let's launch a container using the vagrant environment, which we covered in the last chapter:

```
[russ@mac ~]$ cd ~/Documents/Projects/monitoring-docker/vagrant-centos/
[russ@mac ~]$ vagrant up
Bringing machine 'default' up with 'virtualbox' provider...
==> default: Importing base box 'russmckendrick/centos71'...
==> default: Matching MAC address for NAT networking...
==> default: Checking if box 'russmckendrick/centos71' is up to date...

.....

==> default: => Installing docker-engine ...
==> default: => Configuring vagrant user ...
==> default: => Starting docker-engine ...
==> default: => Installing docker-compose ...
==> default: => Finished installation of Docker
[russ@mac ~]$ vagrant ssh
```

Now that you are connected to the vagrant server, launch the container using the Docker compose file in /monitoring_docker/Chapter01/01-basic/:

```
[vagrant@centos7 ~]$ cd /monitoring_docker/Chapter01/01-basic/
[vagrant@centos7 01-basic]$ docker-compose up -d
Creating 01basic_web_1...
```

You have now pulled down and launched a container in the background. The container is called 01basic_web_1 and it runs NGINX and PHP serving a single PHP information page (http://php.net/manual/en/function.phpinfo.php).

To check whether everything has been launched as expected, run docker-compose ps. You should see your single container with State of Up:

```
[vagrant@centos7 01-basic]$ docker-compose ps
      Name            Command         State         Ports
--------------------------------------------------------------

01basic_web_1   /usr/local/bin/run    Up      0.0.0.0:80->80/tcp
```

Finally, you should be able to see the page containing the output of the PHP information at `http://192.168.33.10/` (this IP address is hardcoded into the vagrant configuration), if you put it in your local browser:

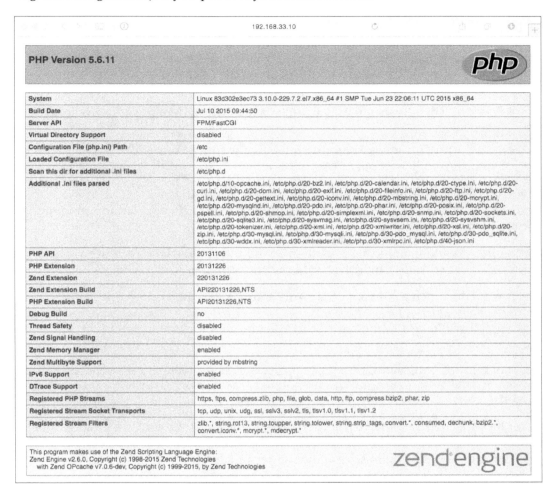

Now, you have a container up and running; let's look at some of the basic stats. We know from the output of `docker-compose` that our container is called `01basic_web_1`, so enter the following command to start streaming statistics in your terminal:

```
docker stats 01basic_web_1
```

It will take a second to initiate; after this is done, you should see your container listed along with the statistics for the following:

- CPU %: This shows you how much of the available CPU resource the container is currently using.

- MEM USEAGE/LIMIT: This tells you how much RAM the container is utilizing; it also displays how much allowance the container has. If you haven't explicitly set a limit, it will show the total amount of RAM on the host machine.

- MEM %: This shows you what percentage of the RAM allowance the container is using.

- NET I/O: This gives a running total of how much bandwidth has been transferred in and out of the container.

If you go back to your browser window and start to refresh http://192.168.33.10/, you will see that the values in each of the columns start to change. To stop streaming the statistics, press *Ctrl + c*.

Rather than keeping on hitting refresh over and over again, let's generate a lot of traffic to 01basic_web_1, which should put the container under a heavy load.

Here, we will launch a container that will send 10,000 requests to 01basic_web_1 using ApacheBench (https://httpd.apache.org/docs/2.2/programs/ab.html). Although it will take a minute or two to execute, we should run docker stats as soon as possible:

```
docker run -d --name=01basic_load --link=01basic_web_1 russmckendrick/ab
ab -k -n 10000 -c 5 http://01basic_web_1/ && docker stats 01basic_web_1
01basic_load
```

After the ApacheBench image has been downloaded and the container that will be called 01basic_load starts, you should see the statistics for both 01basic_web_1 and 01basic_load begin to stream in your terminal:

```
CONTAINER       CPU %     MEM USAGE/LIMIT     MEM %     NET I/O
01basic_load    18.11%    12.71 MB/1.905 GB   0.67%     335.2 MB/5.27 MB
01basic_web_1 139.62%     96.49 MB/1.905 GB   5.07%     5.27 MB/335.2 MB
```

After a while, you will notice that most of the statistics for 01basic_load will drop off to zero; this means that the test has completed and that the container running the test has exited. The docker stats command can only stream statistics for the running containers; ones that have exited are no longer running and, therefore, do not produce output when running docker stats.

Exit from `docker stats` using *Ctrl + c*; to see the results of the ApacheBench command, you can type `docker logs 01basic_load`; you should see something like the following screenshot:

```
[vagrant@centos7 01-basic]$ docker logs 01basic_load
This is ApacheBench, Version 2.3 <$Revision: 1430300 $>
Copyright 1996 Adam Twiss, Zeus Technology Ltd, http://www.zeustech.net/
Licensed to The Apache Software Foundation, http://www.apache.org/

Benchmarking 01basic_web_1 (be patient)
Completed 1000 requests
Completed 2000 requests
Completed 3000 requests
Completed 4000 requests
Completed 5000 requests
Completed 6000 requests
Completed 7000 requests
Completed 8000 requests
Completed 9000 requests
Completed 10000 requests
Finished 10000 requests


Server Software:        nginx/1.8.0
Server Hostname:        01basic_web_1
Server Port:            80

Document Path:          /
Document Length:        90841 bytes

Concurrency Level:      5
Time taken for tests:   14.994 seconds
Complete requests:      10000
Failed requests:        9964
   (Connect: 0, Receive: 0, Length: 9964, Exceptions: 0)
Write errors:           0
Keep-Alive requests:    0
Total transferred:      910057704 bytes
HTML transferred:       908437704 bytes
Requests per second:    666.95 [#/sec] (mean)
Time per request:       7.497 [ms] (mean)
Time per request:       1.499 [ms] (mean, across all concurrent requests)
Transfer rate:          59274.09 [Kbytes/sec] received

Connection Times (ms)
              min  mean[+/-sd] median   max
Connect:        0    0   0.1      0       2
```

You shouldn't worry if you see any failures like in the preceding output. This exercise was purely to demonstrate how to view the statistics of the running containers and not to tune a web server to handle the amount of traffic we sent to it using ApacheBench.

To remove the containers that we launched, run the following commands:

```
[vagrant@centos7 01-basic]$ docker-compose stop
Stopping 01basic_web_1...
[vagrant@centos7 01-basic]$ docker-compose rm
Going to remove 01basic_web_1
Are you sure? [yN] y
Removing 01basic_web_1...
[vagrant@centos7 01-basic]$ docker rm 01basic_load
01basic_load
```

To check whether everything has been removed successfully, run `docker ps -a` and you should not be able to see any running or exited containers that have `01basic_` in their names.

What just happened?

While running the ApacheBench test, you may have noticed that the CPU utilization on the container running NGINX and PHP was high; in the example in the previous section, it was using 139.62 percent of the available CPU resource.

As we did not attach any resource limits to the containers we launched, it was easy for our test to use all of the available resources on the host **Virtual Machine (VM)**. If this VM was being used by several users, all running their own containers, they may have started to notice that their applications had started to slow down or, even worse, the applications had started showing errors.

If you ever find yourself in this situation, you can use `docker stats` to help track down the culprit.

Running `docker stats $(docker ps -q)` will stream the statistics for all the currently running containers:

CONTAINER	CPU %	MEM USAGE/LIMIT	MEM %	NET I/O
361040b7b33e	0.07%	86.98 MB/1.905 GB	4.57%	2.514 kB/738 B
56b459ae9092	120.06%	87.05 MB/1.905 GB	4.57%	2.772 kB/738 B
a3de616f84ba	0.04%	87.03 MB/1.905 GB	4.57%	2.244 kB/828 B
abdbee7b5207	0.08%	86.61 MB/1.905 GB	4.55%	3.69 kB/738 B
b85c49cf740c	0.07%	86.15 MB/1.905 GB	4.52%	2.952 kB/738 B

As you may have noticed, this displays the container ID rather than the name; this information should, however, be enough to spot the resource hog so that you can quickly stop it:

```
[vagrant@centos7 01-basic]$ docker stop 56b459ae9092
56b459ae9092
```

Once stopped, you can then get the name of the rogue container by running the following command:

```
[vagrant@centos7 01-basic]$ docker ps -a | grep 56b459ae9092
```

```
56b459ae9092          russmckendrick/nginx-php    "/usr/local/bin/run" 9
minutes ago         Exited (0) 26 seconds ago      my_bad_container
```

Alternatively, for more detailed information, you can run `docker inspect` `56b459ae9092`, which will give you all the information you need on the container.

What about processes?

One of the great things about Docker is that it isn't really virtualization; as mentioned in the previous chapter, it is a great way of isolating processes rather than running an entire operating system.

This can get confusing when running tools such as `top` or `ps`. To get an idea just how confusing this can get, lets launch several containers using `docker-compose` and see for ourselves:

```
[vagrant@centos7 ~]$ cd /monitoring_docker/Chapter01/02-multiple

[vagrant@centos7 02-multiple]$ docker-compose up -d

Creating 02multiple_web_1...

[vagrant@centos7 02-multiple]$ docker-compose scale web=5

Creating 02multiple_web_2...

Creating 02multiple_web_3...

Creating 02multiple_web_4...

Creating 02multiple_web_5...

Starting 02multiple_web_2...

Starting 02multiple_web_3...

Starting 02multiple_web_4...

Starting 02multiple_web_5...
```

Now, we have five web servers that have all been launched from the same image using the same configuration. One of the first things I do when logging into a server to troubleshoot a problem is run `ps -aux`; this will show all the running processes. As you can see, when running the command, there are a lot processes listed.

Even just trying to look at the processes for NGINX is confusing, as there is nothing to differentiate the processes from one container to another, as shown in the following output:

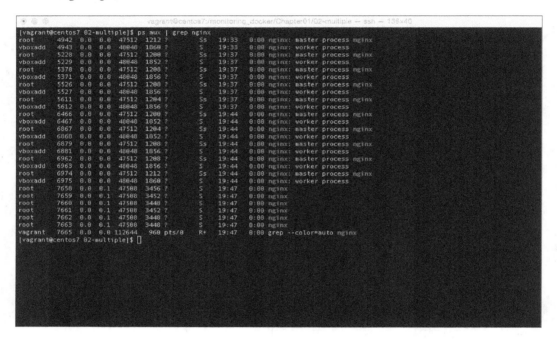

So, how can you know which container owns which processes?

Docker top

This command lists all the processes that are running within a container; think of it as a way of filtering the output of the `ps aux` command we ran on the host machine:

```
[vagrant@centos7 02-multiple]$ docker-compose ps
      Name              Command          State      Ports
--------------------------------------------------------------------------------
02multiple_web_1   /usr/local/bin/run    Up     0.0.0.0:32772->80/tcp
02multiple_web_2   /usr/local/bin/run    Up     0.0.0.0:32773->80/tcp
02multiple_web_3   /usr/local/bin/run    Up     0.0.0.0:32774->80/tcp
02multiple_web_4   /usr/local/bin/run    Up     0.0.0.0:32775->80/tcp
02multiple_web_5   /usr/local/bin/run    Up     0.0.0.0:32776->80/tcp
[vagrant@centos7 02-multiple]$ docker top 02multiple_web_3
UID          PID             PPID           C        STIME       TTY         TIME
    CMD
root         6749            4412           0        19:44       ?           00:00:00
    /usr/bin/python /usr/bin/supervisord -n
root         6877            6749           0        19:44       ?           00:00:00
    php-fpm: master process (/etc/php-fpm.conf)
root         6879            6749           0        19:44       ?           00:00:00
    nginx: master process nginx
vboxadd      6881            6879           0        19:44       ?           00:00:00
    nginx: worker process
666          6900            6877           0        19:44       ?           00:00:00
    php-fpm: pool www
666          6901            6877           0        19:44       ?           00:00:00
    php-fpm: pool www
666          6902            6877           0        19:44       ?           00:00:00
    php-fpm: pool www
666          6903            6877           0        19:44       ?           00:00:00
    php-fpm: pool www
666          6904            6877           0        19:44       ?           00:00:00
    php-fpm: pool www
root         6955            6749           0        19:44       ?           00:00:00
    /usr/libexec/postfix/master -w
postfix      6959            6955           0        19:44       ?           00:00:00
    pickup -l -t unix -u
postfix      6960            6955           0        19:44       ?           00:00:00
    qmgr -l -t unix -u
root         8945            6749           0        19:54       ?           00:00:00
    nginx
[vagrant@centos7 02-multiple]$ []
```

As `docker top` is an implementation of the standard `ps` command, any flags you would normally pass to `ps` should work as follows:

```
[vagrant@centos7 02-multiple]$ docker top 02multiple_web_3 –aux
```

```
[vagrant@centos7 02-multiple]$ docker top 02multiple_web_3 -faux
```

Docker exec

Another way to view what is going on within a container is to enter it. To enable you to do this, Docker introduced the `docker exec` command. This allows you to spawn an additional process within an already running container and then attach to the process; so, if we wanted to look at what is currently running on `02multiple_web_3`, we should use the following command spawn a bash shell within an already running container:

```
docker exec -t -i 02multiple_web_3 bash
```

Once you have an active shell on the container, you will notice that your prompt has changed to the container's ID. Your session is now isolated to the container's environment, meaning that you will only be able to interact with the processes belonging to the container you entered.

From here, you can run the `ps aux` or `top` command as you would do on the host machine, and only see the processes associated with the container you are interested in:

```
●●●                vagrant@centos7:/monitoring_docker/Chapter01/02-multiple — ssh — 136×40
[vagrant@centos7 02-multiple]$ docker exec -t -i 02multiple_web_3 bash
[root@31eb3b9c9217 /]# ps aux
USER       PID %CPU %MEM    VSZ   RSS TTY      STAT START   TIME COMMAND
root         1  0.1  0.6 115252 12672 ?       Ss   18:44   0:00 /usr/bin/python /usr/bin/supervisord -n
root        16  0.0  1.3 377896 25244 ?       S    18:44   0:00 php-fpm: master process (/etc/php-fpm.conf)
root        18  0.0  0.0  47512  1208 ?       Ss   18:44   0:00 nginx: master process nginx
nginx       20  0.0  0.0  48048  1856 ?       S    18:44   0:00 nginx: worker process
webserv+    39  0.0  0.3 377896  6984 ?       S    18:44   0:00 php-fpm: pool www
webserv+    40  0.0  0.3 377896  6984 ?       S    18:44   0:00 php-fpm: pool www
webserv+    41  0.0  0.3 377896  6984 ?       S    18:44   0:00 php-fpm: pool www
webserv+    42  0.0  0.3 377896  6984 ?       S    18:44   0:00 php-fpm: pool www
webserv+    43  0.0  0.3 377896  6988 ?       S    18:44   0:00 php-fpm: pool www
root        94  0.0  0.1  91084  2084 ?       Ss   18:44   0:00 /usr/libexec/postfix/master -w
postfix     95  0.0  0.2  91188  3888 ?       S    18:44   0:00 pickup -l -t unix -u
postfix     96  0.0  0.2  91256  3912 ?       S    18:44   0:00 qmgr -l -t unix -u
root       359  0.2  0.1  13340  1800 ?       Ss   18:57   0:00 bash
root       377  0.0  0.0  21364  1376 ?       R+   18:58   0:00 ps aux
[root@31eb3b9c9217 /]# exit
exit
[vagrant@centos7 02-multiple]$ []
```

To leave the container, type in `exit`, you should see your prompt change back in your host machine.

Finally, you can stop and remove the containers by running `docker-compose stop` and `docker-compose kill`.

Summary

In this chapter, we saw how we can get real-time statistics on our running containers and how we can use commands that are familiar to us, to get information on the processes that are launched as part of each container.

On the face of it, `docker stats` seems like a really basic piece of functionality that isn't really anything more than a tool to help you identify which container is using all the resources while a problem is occurring. However, the Docker command is actually pulling the information from a quite powerful API.

This API forms the basis for a lot of the monitoring tools we will be looking at in the next few chapters.

3
Advanced Container Resource Analysis

In the last chapter, we looked at how you can use the API built into Docker to gain an insight to what resources your containers are running. Now, we are to see how we can take it to the next level by using cAdvisor from Google. In this chapter, you will cover the following topics:

- How to install cAdvisor and start collecting metrics
- Learn all about the web interface and real-time monitoring
- What your options are for shipping metrics to a remote Prometheus database for long-term storage and trend analysis

What is cAdvisor?

Google describes cAdvisor as follows:

> "cAdvisor (Container Advisor) provides container users an understanding of the resource usage and performance characteristics of their running containers. It is a running daemon that collects, aggregates, processes, and exports information about running containers. Specifically, for each container, it keeps resource isolation parameters, historical resource usage, histograms of complete historical resource usage, and network statistics. This data is exported by a container and is machine-wide."

The project started off life as an internal tool at Google for gaining an insight into containers that had been launched using their own container stack.

Google's own container stack was called "Let Me Contain That For You" or lmctfy for short. The work on lmctfy has been installed as a Google port functionality over to libcontainer that is part of the Open Container Initiative. Further details on lmctfy can be found at `https://github.com/google/lmctfy/`.

cAdvisor is written in Go (`https://golang.org`); you can either compile your own binary or you can use the pre-compiled binary that are supplied via a container, which is available from Google's own Docker Hub account. You can find this at `http://hub.docker.com/u/google/`.

Once installed, cAdvisor will sit in the background and capture metrics that are similar to that of the `docker stats` command. We will go through these stats and understand what they mean later in this chapter.

cAdvisor takes these metrics along with those for the host machine and exposes them via a simple and easy-to-use built-in web interface.

Running cAdvisor using a container

There are a number of ways to install cAdvisor; the easiest way to get started is to download and run the container image that contains a copy of a precompiled cAdvisor binary.

Before running cAdvisor, let's launch a fresh vagrant host:

```
[russ@mac ~]$ cd ~/Documents/Projects/monitoring-docker/vagrant-centos/
[russ@mac ~]$ vagrant up
Bringing machine 'default' up with 'virtualbox' provider...
==>default: Importing base box 'russmckendrick/centos71'...
==>default: Matching MAC address for NAT networking...
==>default: Checking if box 'russmckendrick/centos71' is up to date...

. . . . .

==>default: => Installing docker-engine ...
==>default: => Configuring vagrant user ...
==>default: => Starting docker-engine ...
==>default: => Installing docker-compose ...
==>default: => Finished installation of Docker
[russ@mac ~]$ vagrantssh
```

Using a backslash

As we have a lot options to pass to the `docker run` command, we are using \ to split the command over multiple lines so it's easier to follow what is going on.

Once you have access to the host machine, run the following command:

```
docker run \
  --detach=true \
  --volume=/:/rootfs:ro \
  --volume=/var/run:/var/run:rw \
  --volume=/sys:/sys:ro \
  --volume=/var/lib/docker/:/var/lib/docker:ro \
  --publish=8080:8080 \
  --privileged=true \
  --name=cadvisor \
google/cadvisor:latest
```

You should now have a cAdvisor container up and running on your host machine. Before we start, let's look at cAdvisor in more detail by discussing why we have passed all the options to the container.

The cAdvisor binary is designed to run on the host machine alongside the Docker binary, so by launching cAdvisor in a container, we are actually isolating the binary in its down environment. To give cAdvisor access to the resources it requires on the host machine, we have to mount several partitions and also give the container privileged access to let the cAdvisor binary think it is being executed on the host machine.

When a container is launched with `--privileged`, Docker will enable full access to devices on the host machine; also, Docker will configure both AppArmor or SELinux to allow your container the same access to the host machine as a process running outside the container will have. For information on the `--privileged` flag, see this post on the Docker blog at `http://blog.docker.com/2013/09/docker-can-now-run-within-docker/`.

Compiling cAdvisor from source

As mentioned in the previous section, cAdvisor really ought to be executed on the host machine; this means, you may have to use a case to compile your own cAdvisor binary and run it directly on the host.

To compile cAdvisor, you will need to perform the following steps:

1. Install Go and Mercurial on the host machine — version 1.3 or higher of Go is needed to compile cAdvisor.
2. Set the path for Go to work from.
3. Grab the source code for cAdvisor and godep.
4. Set the path for your Go binaries.
5. Build the cAdvisor binary using godep to source the dependencies for us.
6. Copy the binary to /usr/local/bin/.
7. Download either an Upstart or Systemd script and launch the process.

If you followed the instructions in the previous section, you will already have a cAdvisor process running. Before compiling from source, you should start with a clean host; let's log out of the host and launch a fresh copy:

```
[vagrant@centos7 ~]$ exit
logout
Connection to 127.0.0.1 closed.
[russ@mac ~]$ vagrant destroy
default: Are you sure you want to destroy the 'default' VM? [y/N] y
==>default: Forcing shutdown of VM...
==>default: Destroying VM and associated drives...
==>default: Running cleanup tasks for 'shell' provisioner...
[russ@mac ~]$ vagrant up
Bringing machine 'default' up with 'virtualbox' provider...
==>default: Importing base box 'russmckendrick/centos71'...
==>default: Matching MAC address for NAT networking...
==>default: Checking if box 'russmckendrick/centos71' is up to date...


. . . . .


==>default: => Installing docker-engine ...
==>default: => Configuring vagrant user ...
```

```
==>default: => Starting docker-engine ...
==>default: => Installing docker-compose ...
==>default: => Finished installation of Docker
[russ@mac ~]$ vagrantssh
```

To build cAdvisor on the CentOS 7 host, run the following command:

```
sudo yum install -y golanggit mercurial
export GOPATH=$HOME/go
go get -d github.com/google/cadvisor
go get github.com/tools/godep
export PATH=$PATH:$GOPATH/bin
cd $GOPATH/src/github.com/google/cadvisor
godep go build .
sudocpcadvisor /usr/local/bin/
sudowgethttps://gist.githubusercontent.com/russmckendrick/
f647b2faad5d92c96771/raw/86b01a044006f85eebbe395d3857de1185ce4701/
cadvisor.service -O /lib/systemd/system/cadvisor.service
sudosystemctl enable cadvisor.service
sudosystemctl start cadvisor
```

On the Ubuntu 14.04 LTS host, run the following command:

```
sudo apt-get -y install software-properties-common
sudo add-apt-repository ppa:evarlast/golang1.4
sudo apt-get update


sudo apt-get -y install golang mercurial


export GOPATH=$HOME/go
go get -d github.com/google/cadvisor
go get github.com/tools/godep
export PATH=$PATH:$GOPATH/bin
cd $GOPATH/src/github.com/google/cadvisor
godep go build .
sudocpcadvisor /usr/local/bin/
sudowgethttps://gist.githubusercontent.com/russmckendrick/
f647b2faad5d92c96771/raw/e12c100d220d30c1637bedd0ce1c18fb84beff77/
cadvisor.conf -O /etc/init/cadvisor.conf
sudo start cadvisor
```

You should now have a running cAdvisor process. You can check this by running `ps aux | grep cadvisor` and you should see a process with a path of `/usr/local/bin/cadvisor` running.

Collecting metrics

Now, you have cAdvisor running; what do you need to do to configure the service in order to start collecting metrics? The short answer is, nothing at all. When you started the cAdvisor process, it instantly started polling your host machine to find out what containers are running and gathered information on both the running containers and your host machine.

The Web interface

cAdvisor should be running on the `8080` port; if you open `http://192.168.33.10:8080/`, you should be greeted with the cAdvisor logo and an overview of your host machine:

This initial page streams live stats about the host machine, though each section is repeated when you start to drill down and view the containers. To start with, let's look at each section using the host information.

Overview

This overview section gives you a bird's-eye view of your system; it uses gauges so you can quickly get an idea of which resources are reaching their limits. In the following screenshot, there is very little in the way of CPU utilization and the file system usage is relatively low; however, we are using 64% of the available RAM:

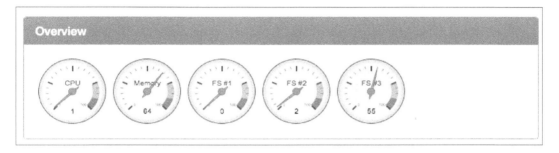

Processes

The following screenshot displays a combined view of the output of the ps aux, dockerps and top commands we used in the previous chapter:

User	PID	PPID	Start Time	CPU %	MEM %	RSS	Virtual Size	Status	Running T
root	4807	4411	19:42	1.20	1.30	25.38 KiB	359.63 KiB	Ssl	00:00
root	4424	2	19:41	0.50	0.00	0.00 B	0.00 B	S<	00:00
root	6	2	19:40	0.20	0.00	0.00 B	0.00 B	S	00:00
root	4411	1	19:41	0.20	1.50	27.52 KiB	654.76 KiB	Ssl	00:00
root	1	0	19:40	0.10	0.20	3.83 KiB	52.89 KiB	Ss	00:00
root	47	2	19:40	0.10	0.00	0.00 B	0.00 B	S	00:00
root	2	0	19:40	0.00	0.00	0.00 B	0.00 B	S	00:00
root	20	2	19:40	0.00	0.00	0.00 B	0.00 B	S<	00:00
root	21	2	19:40	0.00	0.00	0.00 B	0.00 B	S	00:00
root	22	2	19:40	0.00	0.00	0.00 B	0.00 B	S<	00:00
root	23	2	19:40	0.00	0.00	0.00 B	0.00 B	S<	00:00

◄ ► 1 2 3 4

Here is what each column heading means:

- **User**: This shows which user is running the process
- **PID**: This is the unique process ID
- **PPID**: This is the **PID** of the parent process
- **Start Time**: This shows what time the process started
- **CPU %**: This is the percentage of the CPU the process is currently consuming
- **MEM %**: This is the percentage of the RAM the process is currently consuming
- **RSS**: This shows how much of the main memory the process is using
- **Virtual Size**: This shows how much of the virtual memory the process is using
- **Status**: This shows the current status of the process; this are the standard Linux process state codes
- **Running Time**: This shows how long the process has been running
- **Command**: This shows which command the process is running
- **Container**: This shows which container the process is attached to; the container listed as / is the host machine

As there could be several hundred processes active, this section is split into pages; you can navigate to these with the buttons on the bottom-left. Also, you can sort the processes by clicking on any of the headings.

CPU

The following graph shows the CPU utilization over the last minute:

Here is what each term means:

- **Total Usage**: This shows an aggregate usage across all cores
- **Usage per Core**: This graph breaks down the usage per core
- **Usage Breakdown** (not shown in the preceding screenshot): This shows aggregate usage across all cores, but breaks it down to what is being used by the kernel and what is being used by the user-owned processes

Memory

The **Memory** section is split into two parts. The graph tells you the total amount of memory used by all the processes for the host or container; this is the total of the hot and cold memory. The **Hot** memory is the current working set: pages that have been touched by the kernel recently. The **Cold** memory is the page that hasn't been touched for a while and could be reclaimed if needed.

The **Usage Breakdown** gives a visual representation of the total memory in the host machine, or allowance in the container, alongside the total and hot usage:

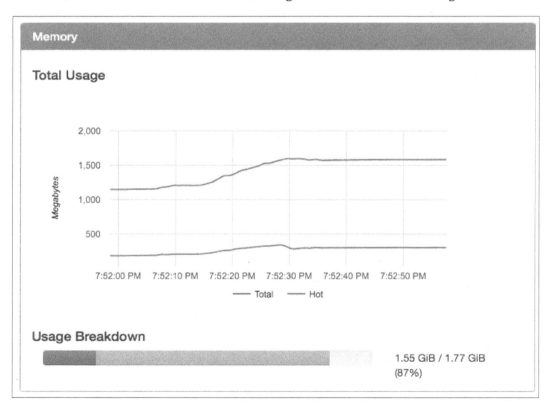

Network

This section shows the incoming and outgoing traffic over the last minute. You can change the interface using the drop-down box on the top-left. There is also a graph that shows any networking errors. Typically, this graph should be flat. If it isn't, then you will be seeing performance issues with your host machine or container:

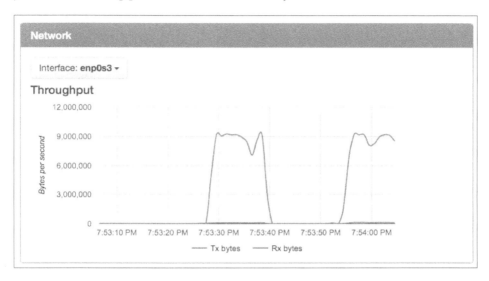

Filesystem

The final section gives a break down of the filesystem usage. In the following screenshot, /dev/sda1 is the boot partition, /dev/sda3 is the main filesystem, and /dev/mapper/docker-8... is an aggregate of the write file systems of your running containers:

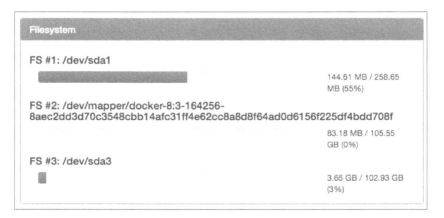

Viewing container stats

At the top of the page, there is a link of your running containers; you can either click on the link or go directly to `http://192.168.33.10:8080/docker/`. Once the page loads, you should see a list of all your running containers, and also a detailed overview of your Docker process, and finally a list of the images you have downloaded.

Subcontainers

Subcontainers shows a list of your containers; each entry is a clickable link that will take you to a page that will give you the following details:

- Isolation:
    - **CPU**: This shows you the CPU allowances of the container; if you have not set any resource limits, you will see the host's CPU information
    - **Memory**: This shows you the memory allowances of the container; if you have not set any resource limits, your container will show an unlimited allowance

- Usage:
    - **Overview**: This shows gauges so you can quickly see how close to any resource limits you are
    - **Processes**: This shows the processes for just your selected container
    - **CPU**: This shows the CPU utilization graphs isolated to just your container
    - **Memory**: This shows the memory utilization of your container

Driver status

The driver gives the basic stats on your main Docker process, along with the information on the host machine's kernel, host name, and also the underlying operating system.

It also gives information on the total number of containers and images. You may notice that the total number of images is a much larger figure than you expected to see; this is because it is counting each file system as an individual image.

For more details on Docker images, see the Docker user guide at `https://docs.docker.com/userguide/dockerimages/`.

It also gives you a detailed breakdown of your storage configuration.

Images

Finally, you get a list of the Docker images which are available on the host machine. It lists the Repository, Tag, Size, and when the image was created, along with the images' unique ID. This lets you know where the image originated from (Repository), which version of the image you have downloaded (Tag) and how big the image is (Size).

This is all great, what's the catch?

So you are maybe thinking to yourself that all of this information available in your browser is really useful; being able to see real-time performance metrics in an easily readable format is a really plus.

The biggest drawback of using the web interface for cAdvisor, as you may have noticed, is that it only shows you one minute's worth of metrics; you can quite literally see the information disappearing in real time.

As a pane of glass gives a real-time view into your containers, cAdvisor is a brilliant tool; if you want to review any metrics that are older than one minute, you are out of luck.

That is, unless you configure somewhere to store all of your data; this is where Prometheus comes in.

Prometheus

So what's Prometheus? Its developers describe it as follows:

> *Prometheus is an open-source system's monitoring and alerting toolkit built at SoundCloud. Since its inception in 2012, it has become the standard for instrumenting new services at SoundCloud and is seeing growing external usage and contributions.*

OK, but what does that have to do with cAdvisor? Well, Prometheus has quite a powerful database backend that stores the data it imports as a time series of events.

Wikipedia describes a time series as follows:

> "*A time series is a sequence of data points, typically consisting of successive measurements made over a time interval. Examples of time series are ocean tides, counts of sunspots, and the daily closing value of the Dow Jones Industrial Average. Time series are very frequently plotted via line charts.*"

https://en.wikipedia.org/wiki/Time_series

One of the things cAdvisor does, by default, is expose all the metrics it is capturing on a single page at `/metrics`; you can see this at `http://192.168.33.10:8080/metrics` on our cAdvisor installation. The metrics are updated each time the page is loaded:

```
# HELP container_cpu_system_seconds_total Cumulative system cpu time consumed in seconds.
# TYPE container_cpu_system_seconds_total counter
container_cpu_system_seconds_total{id="/",name="/"} 13.94
container_cpu_system_seconds_total{id="/system.slice",name="/system.slice"} 0.09
container_cpu_system_seconds_total{id="/system.slice/-.mount",name="/system.slice/-.mount"} 0
container_cpu_system_seconds_total{id="/system.slice/NetworkManager-dispatcher.service",name="/system.slice/NetworkManager-dispatcher.service"} 0
container_cpu_system_seconds_total{id="/system.slice/NetworkManager-wait-online.service",name="/system.slice/NetworkManager-wait-online.service"} 0
container_cpu_system_seconds_total{id="/system.slice/NetworkManager.service",name="/system.slice/NetworkManager.service"} 0
container_cpu_system_seconds_total{id="/system.slice/boot.mount",name="/system.slice/boot.mount"} 0
container_cpu_system_seconds_total{id="/system.slice/brandbot.service",name="/system.slice/brandbot.service"} 0
container_cpu_system_seconds_total{id="/system.slice/cpupower.service",name="/system.slice/cpupower.service"} 0
container_cpu_system_seconds_total{id="/system.slice/crond.service",name="/system.slice/crond.service"} 0
container_cpu_system_seconds_total{id="/system.slice/dbus.service",name="/system.slice/dbus.service"} 0
container_cpu_system_seconds_total{id="/system.slice/dbus.socket",name="/system.slice/dbus.socket"} 0
container_cpu_system_seconds_total{id="/system.slice/dev-disk-by\x2did-
ata\x2dVBOX_HARDDISK_VB25363e5b\x2db6742bbf\x2dpart2.swap",name="/system.slice/dev-disk-by\x2did-
ata\x2dVBOX_HARDDISK_VB25363e5b\x2db6742bbf\x2dpart2.swap"} 0
container_cpu_system_seconds_total{id="/system.slice/dev-disk-by\x2duuid-
f9595940\x2d2813\x2d45a1\x2dae5e\x2dc60e7373c342.swap",name="/system.slice/dev-disk-by\x2duuid-
f9595940\x2d2813\x2d45a1\x2dae5e\x2dc60e7373c342.swap"} 0
container_cpu_system_seconds_total{id="/system.slice/dev-sda2.swap",name="/system.slice/dev-sda2.swap"} 0
container_cpu_system_seconds_total{id="/system.slice/docker-4e9c860c475e96935e65028bbf324138fd7f98c1167e9c426f7f5911d0f129a0.scope",name="cadvisor"}
0.05
```

As you can see in the preceding screenshot, this is just a single long page of raw text. The way Prometheus works is that you configure it to scrape the `/metrics` URL at a user-defined interval, let's say every five seconds; the text is in a format that Prometheus understands and it is ingested into the Prometheus's time series database.

What this means is that, using Prometheus's powerful built-in query language, you can start to drill down into your data. Let's look at getting Prometheus up and running.

Launching Prometheus

Like cAdvisor there are several ways you can launch Prometheus. To start with, we will launch a container and inject our own configuration file so that Prometheus knows where our cAdvisor endpoint is:

```
docker run \
  --detach=true \
  --volume=/monitoring_docker/Chapter03/prometheus.yml:/etc/prometheus/
prometheus.yml \
  --publish=9090:9090 \
  --name=prometheus \
prom/prometheus:latest
```

Once you have launched the container, Prometheus will be accessible on the following URL: `http://192.168.33.10:9090`. When you first load the URL, you will be taken to a status page; this gives some basic information on the Prometheus installation. The important part of this page is the list of targets. This lists the URL that Prometheus will be scrapping to capture metrics; you should see your cAdvisor URL listed with a state of **HEALTHY**, as shown in the following screenshot:

Another information page contains the following:

- **Runtime information**: This displays how long Prometheus has been up and polling data, if you have configured an endpoint
- **Build information**: This contains the details of the version of Prometheus that you have been running
- **Configuration**: This is a copy of the configuration file we injected into the container when it was launched
- **Rules**: This is a copy of any rules we injected; these will be used for alerting
- **Startup flags**: This shows all the runtime variables and their values

Querying Prometheus

As we only have a few containers up and running at the moment, let's launch one that runs Redis so we can start to look at the query language built into Prometheus.

We will use the official Redis image for this and as we are only going to use this as an example we won't need to pass it any user variables:

```
docker run --name my-redis-server -d redis
```

We now have a container called `my-redis-server` running. cAdvisor should already be exposing metrics about the container to Prometheus; let's go ahead and see. In the Prometheus web interface, go to the **Graph** link in the menu at the top of the page. Here, you will be presented with a text box into which you can enter your query. To start with, let's look at the CPU usage of the Redis container.

In the box, enter the following:

```
container_cpu_usage_seconds_total{job="cadvisor",name="my-redis-server"}
```

Then, after clicking on **Execute**, you should have two results returned, listed in the **Console** tab of the page. If you remember, cAdvisor records the CPU usage of each of the CPU cores that the container has access to, which is why we have two values returned, one for "cpu00" and one for "cpu01". Clicking on the **Graph** link will show you results over a period of time:

As you can see in the preceding screenshot, we now have access to the usage graphs for the last 25 minutes, which is about how long ago I launched the Redis instance before generating the graph.

Dashboard

Also, when creating one of the graphs using the query tool in the main application, you can install a separate Dashboard application. This runs in a second container that connects to your main Prometheus container using the API as a data source.

Before we start the Dashboard container, we should initialize a SQLite3 database to store our configuration. To ensure that the database is persistent, we will store this on the host machine in /tmp/prom/file.sqlite3:

```
docker run \
  --volume=/tmp/prom:/tmp/prom \
  -e DATABASE_URL=sqlite3:/tmp/prom/file.sqlite3 \
prom/promdash ./bin/rake db:migrate
```

Once we have initialized the database, we can launch the Dashboard application properly:

```
docker run \
  --detach=true \
  --volume=/tmp/prom:/tmp/prom \
  -e DATABASE_URL=sqlite3:/tmp/prom/file.sqlite3 \
  --publish=3000:3000   \
  --name=promdash \
prom/promdash
```

The application should now be accessible at http://192.168.33.10:3000/. The first thing we need to do is set up the data source. To do this, click on the **Servers** link at the top of the screen and then click on **New Server**. Here, you will be asked to provide the details of your Prometheus server. Name the server and enter the following URL:

- **Name**: cAdvisor
- **URL**: http://192.168.33.10:9090
- **Server Type**: Prometheus

Once you click on **Create Server**, you should receive a message saying **Server was successfully created**. Next up, you need to create a `directory`; this is where your dashboards will be stored.

Click on the **Dashboards** link in the top menu and then click on **New directory** and create one called `Test directory`. Now, you are ready to start creating Dashboards. Click on **New Dashboard**, call it **My Dashboard**, place it in `Test directory`. Once you click on **Create Dashboard**, you will be taken to the preview screen.

From here, you can build up dashboards using the control in the top right-hand side of each section. To add data, you simply enter the query you would like to see in the dashboard section:

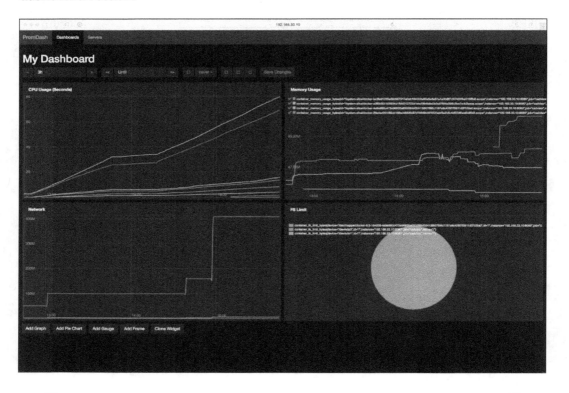

 For detailed information on how to create Dashboards, see the **PROMDASH** section of the Prometheus documentation at `http://prometheus.io/docs/visualization/promdash/`.

The next steps

At the moment, we are running Prometheus in a single container and its data is being stored within that same container. This means, if for any reason the container is terminated, our data is lost; it also means that we can't upgrade without loosing out data. To get around this problem, we can create a data volume container.

 A data volume container is a special type of container that only exists as storage for other containers. For more details, see the Docker user guide at `https://docs.docker.com/userguide/ dockervolumes/#creating-and-mounting-a-data-volume- container`.

First of all, let's make sure we have removed all the running Prometheus containers:

```
docker stop prometheus&&dockerrm Prometheus
```

Next up, let's create a data container called `promdata`:

```
docker create \
  --volume=/promdata \
  --name=promdata \
prom/prometheus /bin/true
```

Finally, launch Prometheus again, this time, using the data container:

```
docker run \
  --detach=true \
  --volumes-from promdata \
  --volume=/monitoring_docker/Chapter03/prometheus.yml:/etc/prometheus/
prometheus.yml \
  --publish=9090:9090 \
  --name=prometheus \
prom/prometheus
```

This will ensure that, if you have to upgrade or relaunch your container, the metrics you have been capturing are safe and sound.

We have only touched on the basics of using Prometheus in this section of the book; for further information on the application, I recommend the following links as a good starting point:

- Documentation: `http://prometheus.io/docs/introduction/overview/`
- Twitter: `https://twitter.com/PrometheusIO`
- Project page: `https://github.com/prometheus/prometheus`
- Google groups: `https://groups.google.com/forum/#!forum/prometheus-developers`

Alternatives?

There are some alternatives to Prometheus. One such alternative is InfluxDB that describes itself as follows:

> *An open-source distributed time series database with no external dependencies.*

However, at the time of writing, cAdvisor is not currently compatible with the latest version of InfluxDB. There are patches in the codebase for cAdvisor; however, these are yet to make it through to the Google-maintained Docker Image.

For more details on InfluxDB and it's new visualization complain application Chronograf, see the project website at `https://influxdb.com/` and for more details on how to export cAdvisor statistics to InfluxDB, see the supporting documentation for cAdvisor at `https://github.com/google/cadvisor/tree/master/docs`.

Summary

In this chapter, we learned how to take the viewing real-time statistics of our containers off the command line and into the web browser. We explored some different methods to install Google's cAdvisor application and also how to use its web interface to keep an eye on our running containers. We also learned how to capture metrics from cAdvisor and store them using Prometheus, a modern time series database.

The two main technologies we have covered in this chapter have only been publically available for less than twelve months. In the next chapter, we will look at using a monitoring tool that has been in a SysAdmins toolbox for over 10 years — Zabbix.

4
A Traditional Approach to Monitoring Containers

So far, we have looked at only a few technologies to monitor our containers, so in this chapter, we will be looking more at a traditional tool for monitoring services. By the end of this chapter, you should know your way around Zabbix and the various ways you can monitor your containers. We will cover the following topics in this chapter:

- How to run a Zabbix Server using containers
- How to launch a Zabbix Server on a vagrant machine
- How to prepare our host system for monitoring containers using the Zabbix agent
- How to find your way around the Zabbix web interface

Zabbix

First things first, what is Zabbix and why use it?

I have personally been using it since version 1.2; the Zabbix site describes it as follows:

> *"With Zabbix, it is possible to gather virtually limitless types of data from the network. High-performance real-time monitoring means that tens of thousands of servers, virtual machines, and network devices can be monitored simultaneously. Along with storing the data, visualization features are available (overviews, maps, graphs, screens, and so on), as well as very flexible ways of analyzing the data for the purpose of alerting.*

Zabbix offers great performance for data gathering and can be scaled to very large environments. Distributed monitoring options are available with the use of Zabbix proxies. Zabbix comes with a web-based interface, secure user authentication, and a flexible user permission schema. Polling and trapping is supported, with native high-performance agents gathering data from virtually any popular operating system; agent-less monitoring methods are available as well."

At the time I started using Zabbix, the only real viable options were as follows:

- Nagios: `https://www.nagios.org/`
- Zabbix: `http://www.zabbix.com/`
- Zenoss: `http://www.zenoss.org/`

Out of the these three options, Zabbix seemed to be the most straightforward one at the time. It was doing enough work to manage the several hundred servers I was going to monitor without having to have the extra work of learning the complexities of setting up Nagios or Zenoss; after all, given the task the software had, I needed to be able to trust that I had set it up correctly.

In this chapter, while I am going to go into some detail about the setup and the basics of using Zabbix, we will only be touching on some of the functionalities, which can do a lot more than just monitor your containers. For more information, I would recommend the following as a good starting point:

- Zabbix blog: `http://blog.zabbix.com`
- Zabbix 2.4 manual: `https://www.zabbix.com/documentation/2.4/manual`
- Further reading: `https://www.packtpub.com/all/?search=zabbix`

Installing Zabbix

As you may have noticed from the links in the previous section, there are a lot of moving parts in Zabbix. It leverages several open source technologies, and a production-ready installation needs a little more planning than we can go into in this chapter. Because of this we are going to look at two ways of installing Zabbix quickly rather go into too much detail.

Using containers

At the time of writing, there are over a hundred Docker images available on the Docker Hub (`https://hub.docker.com`) that mentions Zabbix. These range from full server installations to just the various parts, such as the Zabbix agent or proxy services.

Out of the ones listed, there is one that is recommend by Zabbix itself. So, we will look at this one; it can be found at the following URLs:

- Docker Hub: `https://hub.docker.com/u/zabbix/`
- Project page: `https://github.com/zabbix/zabbix-community-docker`

To get the `ZabbixServer` container up and running, we must first launch a database container. Let's start afresh with our vagrant instance by running the following command:

```
[russ@mac ~]$ cd ~/Documents/Projects/monitoring-docker/vagrant-centos/
[russ@mac ~]$ vagrant destroy
default: Are you sure you want to destroy the 'default' VM? [y/N] y
==>default: Forcing shutdown of VM...
==>default: Destroying VM and associated drives...
==>default: Running cleanup tasks for 'shell' provisioner...
[russ@mac ~]$ vagrant up
Bringing machine 'default' up with 'virtualbox' provider...
==>default: Importing base box 'russmckendrick/centos71'...
==>default: Matching MAC address for NAT networking...
==>default: Checking if box 'russmckendrick/centos71' is up to date...


.....


==>default: => Installing docker-engine ...
==>default: => Configuring vagrant user ...
==>default: => Starting docker-engine ...
==>default: => Installing docker-compose ...
==>default: => Finished installation of Docker
[russ@mac ~]$ vagrantssh
```

Now, we have a clean environment and it's time to launch our database container, as follows:

```
docker run \
  --detach=true \
  --publish=3306 \
  --env="MARIADB_USER=zabbix" \
  --env="MARIADB_PASS=zabbix_password" \
  --name=zabbix-db \
million12/mariadb
```

This will download the `million12/mariadb` image from `https://hub.docker.com/r/million12/mariadb/` and launch a container called `zabbix-db`, running MariaDB 10 (`https://mariadb.org`) with a user called `zabbix` who has a password `zabbix_password`. We have also opened the MariaDB port `3306` up on the container, but as we will be connecting to it from a linked container, there is no need to expose that port on the host machine.

Now, we have the database container up and running, we now need to launch our Zabbix Server container:

```
docker run \
  --detach=true \
  --publish=80:80 \
  --publish=10051:10051 \
  --link=zabbix-db:db \
  --env="DB_ADDRESS=db" \
  --env="DB_USER=zabbix" \
  --env="DB_PASS=zabbix_password" \
  --name=zabbix \
zabbix/zabbix-server-2.4
```

This downloads the image, which at the time of writing is over 1 GB so this process could take several minutes depending on your connection, and launches a container called `zabbix`. It maps the web server (port `80`) and the Zabbix Server process (port `10051`) on the host to the container, creates a link to our database container, sets up the alias `db`, and injects the database credentials as environment variables so that the scripts that launch when the container boots can populate the database.

You can verify that everything worked as expected by checking the logs on the container. To do this, enter `docker logs zabbix`. This will print details of what happened when the container launched on screen:

Now, once we have the container up and running, it is time to move to the browser for our first taste of the web interface. Go to `http://192.168.33.10/` in your browser and you will be greeted by a welcome page; before we can start using Zabbix, we need to complete the installation.

On the welcome page, click on **Next** to be taken to the first step. This will verify that everything we need to run a Zabbix Server is installed. As we have launched it in a container, you should see **OK** next to all of the prerequisites. Click on **Next** to move onto the next step.

Now, we need to configure the database connection for the web interface. Here, you should have the same details as you did when you launched the container, as illustrated in the following screenshot:

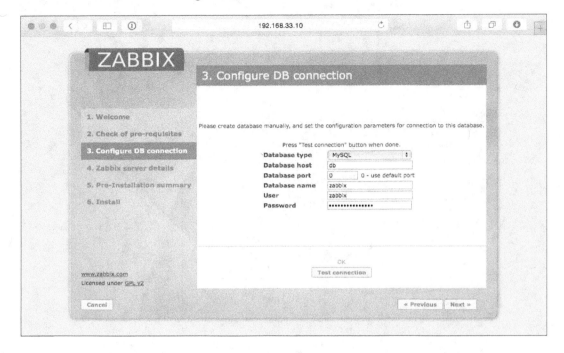

Once you have entered the details, click on **Test connection** and you should receive an **OK** message; you will not be able to proceed until this test completes successfully. Once you have entered the details and have an **OK** message, click on **Next**.

Next up, are the details on the Zabbix Server that the web interface needs to connect to; click on **Next** here. Next up, you will receive a summary of the installation. To proceed, click on **Next** and you will be get confirmation that the /usr/local/src/zabbix/frontends/php/conf/zabbix.conf.php file has been created. Click on **Finish** to be taken to the login page.

Using vagrant

While writing this chapter, I thought a lot about providing another set of installation instructions for the Zabbix Server service. While the book is all about Monitoring Docker containers, having a service as resource intensive as Zabbix running inside a container feels a little counter intuitive. Because of this, there is a vagrant machine that uses Puppet to bootstrap a working installation of Zabbix Server:

```
[russ@mac ~]$ cd ~/Documents/Projects/monitoring-docker/vagrant-zabbix/
[russ@mac ~]$ vagrant up
Bringing machine 'default' up with 'virtualbox' provider...
==>default: Importing base box 'russmckendrick/centos71'...
==>default: Matching MAC address for NAT networking...
==>default: Checking if box 'russmckendrick/centos71' is up to date...

. . . . .

==>default: Debug: Received report to process from zabbix.media-glass.es
==>default: Debug: Evicting cache entry for environment 'production'
==>default: Debug: Caching environment 'production' (ttl = 0 sec)
==>default: Debug: Processing report from zabbix.media-glass.es with
processor Puppet::Reports::Store
```

As you may have noticed, there is a lot of output streamed to the terminal, so what just happened? First of all, a CentOS 7 vagrant instance was launched and then a Puppet agent was installed. Once installed, the installation was handed off to Puppet. Using the Zabbix Puppet module by Werner Dijkerman, Zabbix Server was installed; for more details on the module, see its Puppet Forge page at https://forge.puppetlabs.com/wdijkerman/zabbix.

Unlike the containerized version of Zabbix Server, there is no additional configuration required, so you should be able to access the Zabbix login page at http://zabbix.media-glass.es/ (an IP address of 192.168.33.11 is hardcoded into the configuration).

Preparing our host machine

For the remainder of this chapter, I will assume that you are using the Zabbix Server that is running on its own vagrant instance. This helps to ensure that your environment is consistent with the configuration of the Zabbix agent we will be looking at.

To pass the statistics from our containers to the Zabbix agent, which will then in turn expose them to the Zabbix Server, we will be installing using the Zabbix-Docker-Monitoring Zabbix agent module that has been developed by Jan Garaj. For more information on the project, see the following URLs:

- The Project page: `https://github.com/monitoringartist/Zabbix-Docker-Monitoring/`
- The Zabbix share page: `https://share.zabbix.com/virtualization/docker-containers-monitoring`

To get the agent and module installed, configured, and running, we need to execute the following steps:

1. Install the Zabbix package repository.
2. Install the Zabbix agent.
3. Install the prerequisites for the module.
4. Add the Zabbix agent user to the Docker group.
5. Download the auto-discovery bash script.
6. Download the precompiled `zabbix_module_docker` binary.
7. Configure the Zabbix agent with the details of our Zabbix Server and also the Docker module.
8. Set the correct permissions on all the files we have downloaded and created.
9. Start the Zabbix agent.

While the steps remain the same for both CentOS and Ubuntu, the actions taken to do the initial package installation differ slightly. Rather than going through the process of showing the commands to install and configure the agent, there is a script for each of the host operating systems in the `/monitoring_docker/chapter04/` folder. To view the scripts, run the following command from your terminal:

```
cat /monitoring_docker/chapter04/install-agent-centos.sh
cat /monitoring_docker/chapter04/install-agent-ubuntu.sh
```

Now, you have taken a look at the scripts its time to run them, to do this type one of the following commands. If you are running CentOS, run this command:

```
bash /monitoring_docker/chapter04/install-agent-centos.sh
```

For Ubuntu, run the following command:

```
bash /monitoring_docker/chapter04/install-agent-ubuntu.sh
```

To verify that everything ran as expected, check the Zabbix agent log file by running the following command:

```
cat /var/log/zabbix/zabbix_agentd.log
```

You should see that the end of the file confirms that the agent has started and that the `zabbix_module_docker.so` module has been loaded:

Before we move onto the Zabbix web interface, let's launch a few containers using the `docker-compose` file from *Chapter 2, Using the Built-in Tools*:

```
[vagrant@docker ~]$ cd /monitoring_docker/chapter02/02-multiple/
[vagrant@docker 02-multiple]$ docker-compose up -d
[vagrant@docker 02-multiple]$ docker-compose scale web=3
[vagrant@docker 02-multiple]$ docker-compose ps
```

We should now have three web server containers running and a running Zabbix agent on the host.

The Zabbix web interface

Once you have Zabbix installed you can open the Zabbix web interface by going to `http://zabbix.media-glass.es/` in your browser, this link will only work when you have the Zabbix vagrant box up and running, if you don't have it running the page will time out. You should be presented with a login screen. Enter the default username and password here, which is `Admin` and `zabbix` (note that the username has a capital *A*), to login.

Once logged in, you will need to add the host templates. These are preconfigured environment settings and will add some context around the statistics that the Zabbix agent is sending to the server, along with the auto-discovery of containers.

To add the templates, go to the **Configuration** tab in the top menu and select **Template**; this will bring up a list of all the templates that are currently installed. Click on the **Import** button in the header and upload a copy of the two template files you can find in the `~/Documents/Projects/monitoring-docker/chapter04/ template` folder on your main machine; there is no need to change the rules when uploading the templates.

Once both templates have been successfully imported, it is time to add our Docker host. Again, go to the **Configuration** tab, but this time select **Hosts**. Here, you need to click on **Create host**. Then, enter the following information in the **Host** tab:

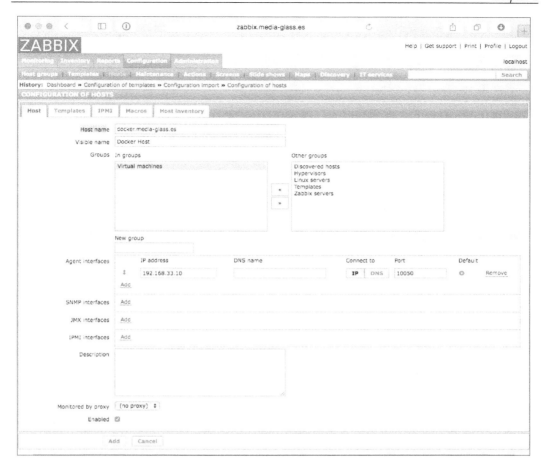

Here are the details of the preceding information:

- **Host name**: This is the host name of our Docker host
- **Visible name**: Here, the name server will appear as in Zabbix
- **Groups**: Which group within Zabbix the server you would like the Docker host to be part of
- **Agent Interfaces**: This is the IP address or the DNS name of our Docker host
- **Enabled**: This should be ticked

Before clicking on **Add**, you should click on the **Templates** tab and link the following two templates to the host:

- **Template App Docker**
- **Template OS Linux**

Here is the screenshot of the host:

Once you have added the two templates, click on **Add** to configure and enable the host. To verify that the host has been added correctly, you should go to the **Monitoring** tab and then **Latest data**. From here, click on **Show filter** and enter the host machine in the **Hosts** box. You should then start to see items appearing:

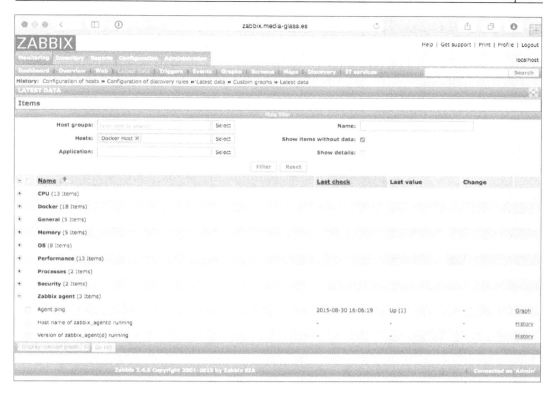

Don't worry if you don't see the **Docker** section immediately, by default, Zabbix will attempt to auto-discover new containers every five minutes.

Docker metrics

For each container, Zabbix discovers the following metrics that will be recorded:

- Container (your Containers name) is running
- CPU system time
- CPU user time
- Used cache memory
- Used RSS memory
- Used swap

Apart from "Used swap", these are the same metrics recorded by cAdvisor.

Create custom graphs

You can access a time-based graph for any of the metrics collected by Zabbix; you can also create your own custom graphs. In the following graph, I have created a graph that plots all the CPU System stats from the three web containers we launched earlier in the chapter:

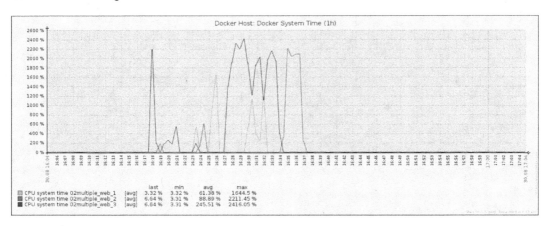

As you can see, I performed a few tests using ApacheBench to make the graph a little more interesting.

For more information on how to create custom graphs, see the graphs section of the documentation site at https://www.zabbix.com/documentation/2.4/manual/config/visualisation/graphs.

Compare containers to your host machine

As we added the Linux OS template and the Docker template to the host and we are also recording quite a lot of information about the system, here we can tell the effect the testing with ApacheBench had on the overall processor load:

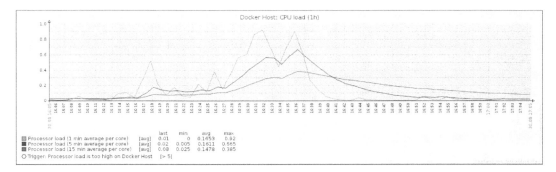

We can drill down further to get information on the overall utilization:

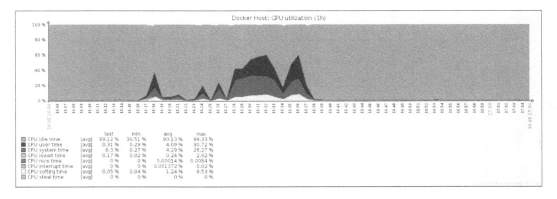

Triggers

Another feature of Zabbix is triggers: you can define actions to happen when a metric meets a certain set of criteria. In the following example, Zabbix has been configured with a trigger called **Container Down**; this changes the status of the monitored item to **Problem** with a severity of **Disaster**:

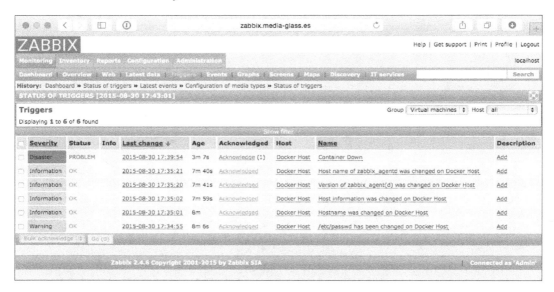

This change in status then triggers an e-mail to inform that, for some reason the container is no longer up and running:

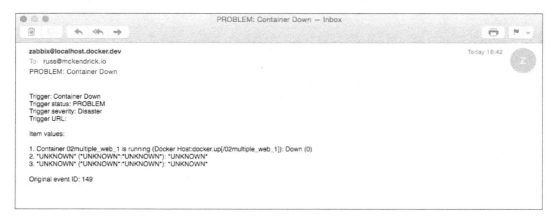

This could have also triggered other tasks, such as running a custom script, sending an instant message via Jabber, or even triggering a third-party service such as PagerDuty (`https://www.pagerduty.com`) or Slack (`https://slack.com`).

For more information on Triggers, Events, and Notifications, see the following sections of the documentation:

- `https://www.zabbix.com/documentation/2.4/manual/config/triggers`
- `https://www.zabbix.com/documentation/2.4/manual/config/events`
- `https://www.zabbix.com/documentation/2.4/manual/config/notifications`

Summary

So, how does this traditional approach to monitoring fit into a container's lifecycle?

Going back to the Pets versus Cattle analogy, at first glance, Zabbix seems to be geared more towards Pets: its feature set is best suited to monitoring services that are static over a long period of time. This means that the same approach to monitoring a pet can also be applied to long-running processes running within your containers.

Zabbix is also the perfect option for monitoring mixed environments. Maybe you have several database servers that are not running as containers, but you have several hosts running Docker, and have equipment such as switches and SANs that you need to monitor. Zabbix can provide you with a single pane of glass showing you metrics for all your environments, along with being able to alert you to problems.

So far, we have looked at using APIs and metrics provided by Docker and LXC, but what about other metrics can we use? In the next chapter, we will look at a tool that hooks straight into the host machine's kernel to gather information on your containers.

Querying with Sysdig

5

The previous tools we have looked at have all relied on making API calls to Docker or reading metrics from LXC. Sysdig works differently by hooking itself into the hosts machine's kernel while this approach does go against Docker's philosophy of each service being run in its own isolated container, the information you can get by running Sysdig only for a few minutes far outweighs any arguments about not using it.

In this chapter, we will look at the following topics:

- How to install Sysdig and Csysdig on the host machine
- Basic usage and how to query your containers in real time
- How to capture logs so they can be queried later

What is Sysdig?

Before we start to get into Sysdig, let's first understand what it is. When I first heard about the tool, I thought to myself that it sounded too good to be true; the website describes the tool as follows:

> *"Sysdig is open source, system-level exploration: capture system state and activity from a running Linux instance, then save, filter and analyze. Sysdig is scriptable in Lua and includes a command line interface and a powerful interactive UI, csysdig, that runs in your terminal. Think of sysdig as strace + tcpdump + htop + iftop + lsof + awesome sauce. With state of the art container visibility on top."*

This is quite a claim as all the tools that it is claiming to be as powerful were all in a set of goto commands to run when looking into problems, so I was a little skeptical at first.

As any one who has had to try and track down a haywire process of try and track down an issue that isn't being very verbose in its error logs on a Linux server will know that using tools such as strace, lsof, and tcpdump can get complicated very quickly and it normally involves capturing a whole lot of data and then using a combination of several tools to slowly, and manually, trace the problem by reducing the amount of data you captured.

Imagine my delight when Sysdig's claims turned out to be true. It made me wish I had the tool back when I was a front line engineer; it would have made my life a lot easier.

Sysdig comes in two different flavors, first is the Open Source version available at http://www.sysdig.org/; this comes with an ncurses interface so that you can easily access and query data from a terminal-based GUI.

 Wikipedia describes **ncurses** (new curses) as a programming library that provides an API that allows the programmer to write text-based user interfaces in a terminal-independent manner. It is a toolkit for developing "GUI-like" application software that runs under a terminal emulator. It also optimizes screen changes in order to reduce the latency experienced when using remote shells.

There is also a commercial service that allows you to stream your Sysdig to their externally hosted service; this version has a web-based interface for viewing and querying your data.

In this chapter, we will be concentrating on the open source version.

Installing Sysdig

Considering how powerful Sysdig is, it has one of the most straightforward installation and configuration processes I have come across. To install Sysdig on either a CentOS or Ubuntu server, type the following command:

```
curl -s https://s3.amazonaws.com/download.draios.com/stable/install-sysdig | sudo bash
```

After running the preceding command, you will get the following output:

That's it, you are ready to go. There is nothing more to configure or do. There is a manual installation process and also a way of installing the tool using containers to build the necessary kernel modules; for more details, see the installation guide as follows:

```
http://www.sysdig.org/wiki/how-to-install-sysdig-for-linux/
```

Using Sysdig

Before we look at how to use Sysdig, let's launch a few containers using `docker-compose` by running the following command:

```
cd /monitoring_docker/chapter05/wordpress/
docker-compose up -d
```

This will launch a WordPress installation running a database and two web server containers that are load balanced using an HAProxy container. You will be able to view the WordPress installation at `http://docker.media-glass.es/` once the containers have launched. You will need to enter some details to create the admin user before the site is visible; follow the on-screen prompts to complete these steps.

The basics

At its core, Sysdig is a tool for producing a stream of data; you can view the stream by typing `sudo sysdig` (to quit, press *Ctrl+c*).

There is a lot information there so let's start to filter the stream down and run the following command:

sudosysdigevt.type=chdir

This will display only events in which a user changes directory; to see it in action, open a second terminal and you will see that when you log in, you see some activity in the first terminal. As you can see, it looks a lot like a traditional log file; we can format output to give information such as the username, by running the following command:

sudosysdig -p"user:%user.name dir:%evt.arg.path" evt.type=chdir

Then, in your second terminal, change the directory a few times:

```
[vagrant@docker ~]$
[vagrant@docker ~]$ sudo sysdig evt.type=chdir
8867 14:53:21.697963484 1 sshd (10824) > chdir
8868 14:53:21.697965885 1 sshd (10824) < chdir res=0 path=/
9238 14:53:21.700103157 0 sshd (10825) > chdir
9239 14:53:21.700105452 0 sshd (10825) < chdir res=0 path=/
14419 14:53:21.741002121 1 sshd (10827) > chdir
14420 14:53:21.741004159 1 sshd (10827) < chdir res=0 path=/home/vagrant
^C[vagrant@docker ~]$ sudo sysdig -p"user:%user.name dir:%evt.arg.path" evt.type=chdir
user:vagrant dir:/tmp
user:vagrant dir:/monitoring_docker
[vagrant@docker ~]$ []
```

As you can see, this is a lot easier to read than the original unformatted output. Press *Ctrl + c* to stop filtering.

Capturing data

In the previous section, we looked at filtering data in real time; it is also possible to stream Sysdig data to a file so that you can query the data at a later time. Exit from your second terminal and run the following command on your first one:

```
sudosysdig -w ~/monitoring-docker.scap
```

While the command is running on the first terminal, log in to the host on the second one and change the directory a few times. Also, while we are recording, click around the WordPress site we started at the beginning of this section, the URL is http://docker.media-glass.es/. Once you have done that, stop the recording by pressing *Crtl + c*; you should have now dropped back to a prompt. You can check the size of the file created by Sysdig by running the following:

```
ls -lha ~/monitoring-docker.scap
```

Now, we can use the data that we have captured to apply the same filter as we did when looking at the real-time stream:

```
sudosysdig -r ~/monitoring-docker.scap -p"user:%user.name dir:%evt.arg.
path" evt.type=chdir
```

By running the preceding command, you will get the following output:

```
[vagrant@docker ~]$ sudo sysdig -w ~/monitoring-docker.scap
^C[vagrant@docker ~]$ ls -lhat ~/monitoring-docker.scap
-rw-r--r-- 1 root root 2.0M Aug 31 15:00 /home/vagrant/monitoring-docker.scap
[vagrant@docker ~]$ sudo sysdig -r ~/monitoring-docker.scap -p"user:%user.name dir:%evt.arg.path" evt.type=chdir
user:root dir:/
user:root dir:/
user:vagrant dir:/home/vagrant
user:vagrant dir:/tmp
user:vagrant dir:/monitoring_docker
[vagrant@docker ~]$
```

Notice how we get similar results to when we were viewing the data in real time.

Containers

One of the things that was recorded in ~/monitoring-docker.scap was details on the system state; this includes information on the containers we launched at the start of the chapter. Let's use this file to get some stats on the containers. To list the containers that were active during the time, we captured the data file run:

```
sudo sysdig -r ~/monitoring-docker.scap -c lscontainers
```

To see which of the containers utilized the CPU most of the time, we were clicking around the WordPress site run:

```
sudo sysdig -r ~/monitoring-docker.scap -c topcontainers_cpu
```

To have a look at the top processes in each of the containers that have "wordpress" in their names (which is all of them in our case), run the following command:

```
sudo sysdig -r ~/monitoring-docker.scap -c topprocs_cpu container.name
contains wordpress
```

Finally, which of our containers transferred the most amount of data?:

```
sudosysdig -r ~/monitoring-docker.scap -c topcontainers_net
```

By running the preceding command, you will get the following output:

As you can see, we have extracted quite a bit of information on our containers from the data we captured. Also, using the file, you can remove the `-r ~/monitoring-docker.scap` part of the command to view the container metrics in real time.

It's also worth pointing out that there are binaries for Sysdig that work on both OS X and Windows; while these do not capture any data, they can be used to read data that you have recorded on your Linux host.

Further reading

From the few basic exercises covered in this section, you should start to get an idea of just how powerful Sysdig can be. There are more examples on the Sysdig website at `http://www.sysdig.org/wiki/sysdig-examples/`. Also, I recommend you to read the blog post at `https://sysdig.com/fishing-for-hackers/`; it was my first exposure to Sysdig and it really demonstrates its usefulness.

Using Csysdig

As easy as it is to view data captured by Sysdig using the command line and manually filtering the results, it can get more complicated as you start to string more and more commands together. To help make the data captured by Sysdig as accessible as possible, Sysdig ships with a GUI called **Csysdig**.

Launching the Csysdig is done with a single command:

```
sudo csysdig
```

Once the process has launched, it should instantly look familiar to anyone who has used top or cAdvisor (minus the graphs); its default view will show you real-time information on the processes that are running:

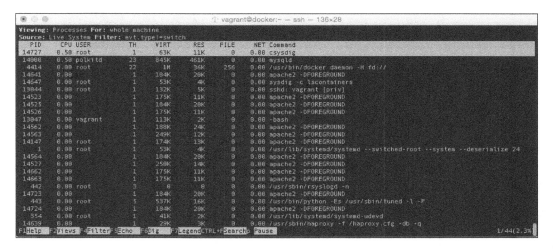

To change this view, known as the **Processes** view, press *F2* to open the **Views** menu; from here, you can use the up and down arrows on your keyboard to select a view. As you may have already guessed, we would like to see the **Containers** view:

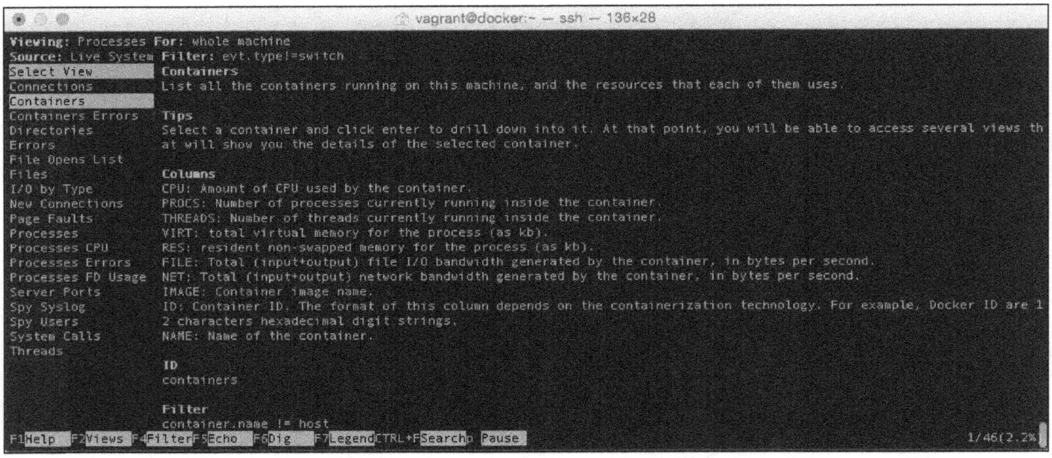

However, before we drill down into our containers, let's quit Csysdig by pressing *q* and load up the file we created in the previous section. To do this, type the following command:

```
sudo csysdig -r ~/monitoring-docker.scap
```

Once Csysdig loads, you will notice that **Source** has changed from **Live System** to the file path of our data file. From here, press *F2* and use the up arrow to select containers and then hit *Enter*. From here, you can use the up and down arrows to select one of the two web servers, these would be either wordpress_wordpress1_1 or wordpress_wordpress2_1 as shown in the following screen:

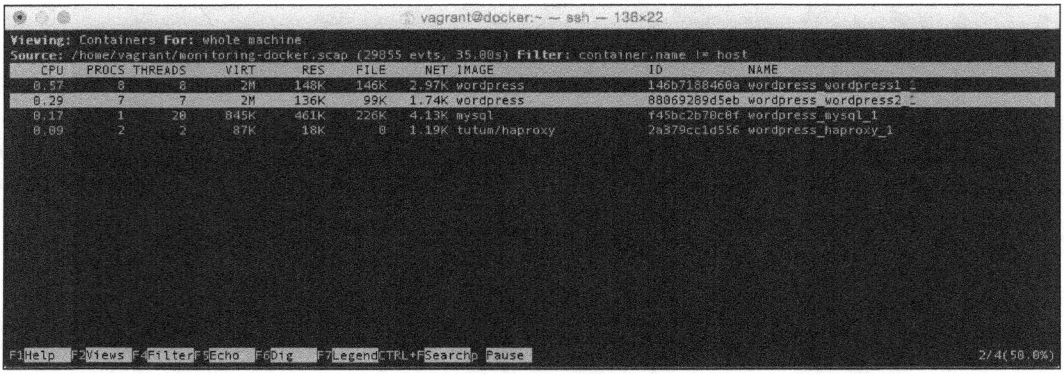

The remaining part of this chapter assumes that you have Csysdig open in-front of you, it will talk you through how to navigate around the tool. Please feel free to explore yourself as well.

Once you have selected a server, hit *Enter* and you will be presented with a list of processes that the container was running. Again, you can use the arrow keys to select a process to drill down further into.

I suggested looking at one of the Apache processes that has a value listed in the **File** column. This time, rather than pressing *Enter* to select the process, let's "Echo" what the process was up to at the time we captured the data; with the process selected, press *F5*.

You can use the up and down arrows to scroll through the output:

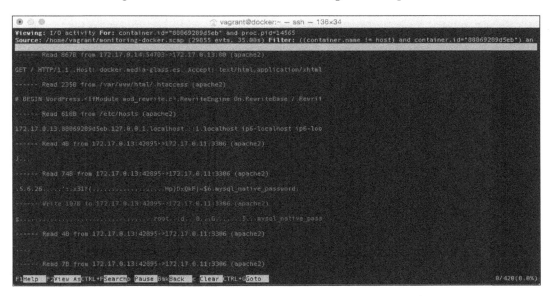

To better format the data, press *F2* and select **Printable ASCII**. As you can see from the preceding screenshot, this Apache process performed the following tasks:

- Accepted an incoming connection
- Accessed the `.htaccess` file
- Read the `mod_rewrite` rules
- Got information from the hosts file
- Made a connection to the MySQL container
- Sent the MySQL password

By scrolling through the remainder of the data in the "Echo" results for the process, you should be able to easily follow the interactions with the database all the way through to the page being sent to the browser.

To leave the "Echo" screen, press *Backspace*; this will always take you a level back.

If you want a more detailed breakdown on what the process was doing, then press *F6* to enter the **Dig** view; this will list the files that the process was accessing at the time, along with the network interaction and how it is accessing the RAM.

To view a full list of commands and for more help, you can press *F1* at anytime. Also, to get a breakdown on any columns that are on screen, press *F7*.

Summary

As I mentioned at the start of this chapter, Sysdig is probably one of the most powerful tools I have come across in recent years.

Part of its power is the way that it exposes a lot of information and metrics in a way that never feels overwhelming. It's clear that the developers have spent a lot of time ensuring that both the UI and the way that commands are structured feel natural and instantly understandable, even by the newest member of an operations team.

The only downside is that, unless you want to view the information in real time or look into a problem in development storing the amount of data that is being generated by Sysdig, it can be quite costly in terms of disc space being used.

This is something that Sysdig has recognized, and to help with this, the company offers a cloud-based commercial service called Sysdig Cloud for you to stream your Sysdig data into. In the next chapter, we will look at this service and also some of its competitors.

Exploring Third Party Options

6

So far, we have been looking at the tools and services you host yourself. Along with these self-hosted tools, a large amount of cloud-based software has developed around Docker as a service ecosystem. In this chapter, we will look at the following topics:

- Why use a SaaS service over self-hosted or real-time metrics?
- What services are available and what do they offer?
- Installation of agents for Sysdig Cloud, Datadog, and New Relic on the host machines
- Configuration of the agents to ship metrics

A word about externally hosted services

So far, to work through the examples in this book, we have used locally hosted virtual servers that are launched using vagrant. During this chapter, we are going to use services that need to be able to communicate with your host machine, so rather than trying to do this using your local machine, its about time you took your host machine into the cloud.

As we are going to start and stop the remote hosts while we look at the services, it pays to use a public cloud, as we only get charged for what we use.

There are several public cloud services that you can use to evaluate the tools covered in this chapter, which one you choose to use is up to you, you could use:

- Digital Ocean: `https://www.digitalocean.com/`
- Amazon Web Services: `https://aws.amazon.com/`
- Microsoft Azure: `https://azure.microsoft.com/`
- VMware vCloud Air: `http://vcloud.vmware.com/`

Or use your own preferred provider, the only pre-requisite is that your server is publically accessible.

This chapter assumes that you are capable of launching either a CentOS 7 or Ubuntu 14.04 cloud instance and you understand that you will likely incur charges while the cloud instance is up and running.

Deploying Docker in the cloud

Once you have launched your cloud instance, you can bootstrap Docker in the same way that you installed using vagrant. In the `chapter 6` folder of the Git repository, there are two separate scripts to download and install the Docker engine and compose it on your cloud instance.

To install Docker, ensure that your cloud instance is updated by running:

```
sudo yum update
```

For the CentOS instance of your Ubuntu, run the following command:

```
sudo apt-get update
```

Once updated, run the following command to install the software. Due to the differences in the way different cloud environments are configured, it is best to switch over to the root user to run the remainder of the commands, to do this, run:

```
sudo su -
```

Now you will be able to run the install script using the following command:

```
curl -fsS https://raw.githubusercontent.com/russmckendrick/monitoring-docker/master/chapter06/install_docker/install_docker.sh | bash
```

To check that everything works as expected, run the following command:

```
docker run hello-world
```

You should see something similar to the terminal output, as shown in the following screenshot:

We can start to look at the SasS services once you have Docker up and running.

Why use a SaaS service?

You may have noticed while working with the examples in the previous chapters that the tools we have used can potentially use many resources if we needed to start collecting more metrics, especially if the applications we want to monitor are in production.

To help shift this load from both storage and CPU, a number of cloud-based SaaS options have started offering support to record metrics for your containers. Many of these services were already offering services to monitor servers, so adding support for containers seemed a natural progression for them.

These typically require you to install an agent on your host machine, once installed, the agent will sit in the background and report to the services, normally cloud-based and API services.

A few of the services allow you to deploy the agents as Docker containers. They offer containerized agents so that the service can run on stripped down operating systems, such as:

- CoreOS: https://coreos.com/
- RancherOS: http://rancher.com/rancher-os/
- Atomic: http://www.projectatomic.io/
- Ubuntu Snappy Core: https://developer.ubuntu.com/en/snappy/

These operating systems differ from traditional ones, as you cannot install services on them directly; their only purpose is to run a service, such as Docker, so that you can launch the services or applications you need to be run as containers.

As we are running full operating systems as our host systems, we do not need this option and will be deploying the agents directly to the hosts.

The SaaS options that we are going to look at in this chapter are as follows:

- Sysdig Cloud: https://sysdig.com/product/
- Datadog: https://www.datadoghq.com/
- New Relic: http://newrelic.com

They all offer free trials and two of them offer free cut-down versions of the main service. On the face of it, they might all appear to offer similar services; however, when you start to use them, you will immediately notice that they are in fact all very different from each other.

Sysdig Cloud

In the previous chapter, we had a look at the open source version of Sysdig. We saw that there is a great ncurses interface called cSysdig and it allows us to navigate through all the data that Sysdig is collecting about our host.

The sheer amount of metrics and data collected by Sysdig means that you have to try to stay on top of it either by shipping your files off the server, maybe to Amazon Simple Storage Service (S3), or to some local shared storage. In addition, you can query the data in the command line on the host itself or on your local machine using an installation of the command-line tools.

This is where Sysdig Cloud comes into play; it offers a web-based interface to the metrics that Sysdig captures along with the options to ship the Sysdig captures off your host machine either to Sysdig's own storage or to your S3 bucket.

Sysdig cloud offers the following functionality:

- ContainerVision™
- Real-Time Dashboard
- Historical Replay
- Dynamic Topology
- Alerting

As well as, the option to trigger a capture on any of your hosts and at any time.

Sysdig describes ContainerVision as:

> *"Sysdig Cloud's patent-pending core technology, ContainerVision, is the only monitoring technology on the market designed specifically to respect the unique characteristics of containers. ContainerVision offers you deep and comprehensive visibility into all aspects of your containerized environment - applications, infrastructures, servers, and networks - all without the need to pollute your containers with any extra instrumentation. In other words, ContainerVision gives you 100% visibility into the activity inside your containers, from the outside."*

Before we delve into Sysdig Cloud any further, I should point out that this is a commercial server and at the time of writing, it costs $25 per host per month. There is also a 14-day fully featured trial available. If you wish to work through the agent installation and follow the example in this chapter, you will need an active account that runs either on the 14-day trial or a paid subscription.

- Sign up for a 14-day free trial: `https://sysdig.com/`
- Details on pricing: `https://sysdig.com/pricing/`
- Introduction to the company: `https://sysdig.com/company/`

Installing the agent

The agent installation is similar to installing the open source version; you need to ensure that your cloud host is running an up-to-date kernel and that you are also booted into the kernel.

Some cloud providers keep a tight control on the kernels you can boot into (for example, Digital Ocean), and they do not allow you to manage your kernel on the host itself. Instead, you need to choose the correct version through their control panel.

Once you have the correct kernel installed, you should be able to run the following command to install the agent. Ensure that you replace the access key at the end of the command with your own access key, which can be found on your **User Profile** page or on the agent installation pages; you can find these at:

- User Profile: `https://app.sysdigcloud.com/#/settings/user`
- Agent Installation: `https://app.sysdigcloud.com/#/settings/agentInstallation`

The command to run is:

```
curl -s https://s3.amazonaws.com/download.draios.com/stable/install-agent
| sudo bash -s -- --access_key wn5AYlhjRhgn3shcjW14y3yOTO9WsF7d
```

The shell output should look like the following screen:

Once the agent has been installed, it will immediately start to report the data back to Sysdig Cloud. If you click on **Explore**, you will see your host machine and the running containers:

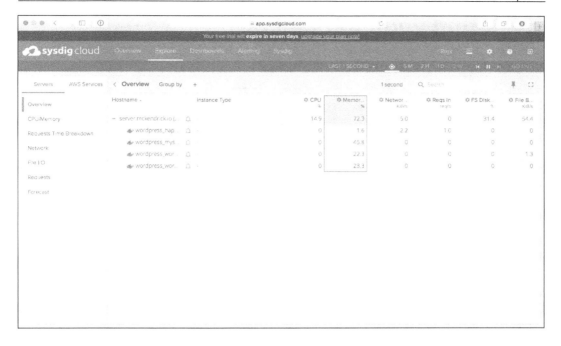

As you can see here, I have my host machine and four containers running a WordPress installation similar to the one we used in the previous chapter. From here, we can start to drill down into our metrics.

To launch the WordPress installation on your cloud-based machine, run the following commands as the root user:

```
sudo su -
```

```
mkdir ~/wordpress
```

```
curl -L https://raw.githubusercontent.com/russmckendrick/monitoring-
docker/master/chapter05/wordpress/docker-compose.yml > ~/wordpress/
docker-compose.yml
```

```
cd ~/wordpress
```

```
docker-compose up -d
```

Exploring your containers

The Sysdig Cloud web interface will feel instantly familiar, as it shares a similar design and overall feeling with cSysdig:

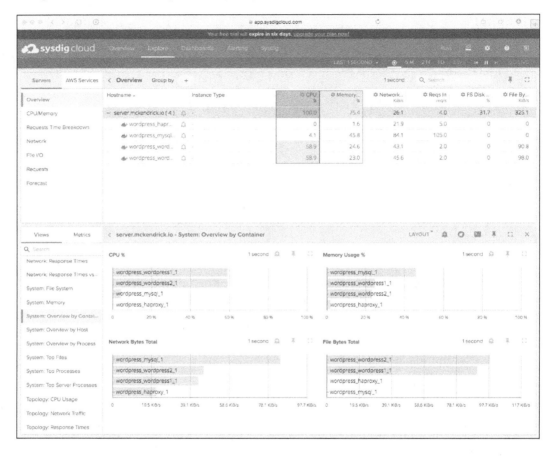

Once you start to drill down, you can see that a bottom pane opens up and this is where you can view the statistics. One of the things I liked about Sysdig Cloud is that it opens up a wealth of metrics and there should be very little that you need to configure from here.

For example, if you want to know what processes have been consuming the most CPU time in the last 2 hours, click on **2H** in the secondary menu and then from the **Views** tab in the bottom-left click on **System: Top Processes**; this will give you a table of the processes, ordered by the ones that have used the most time.

To apply this view to a container, click on a container in the top-section and the bottom-section will be instantly updated to reflect the top CPU utilization for just that container; as most containers will only run one or two processes, this may not be that interesting. So, let's have a deep look at the processes themselves. Let's say, we clicked on our database container and we wanted information on what is happening within MySQL.

Sysdig Cloud comes with application overlays, these when selected give you more granular information on the processes within the container. Selecting the **App: MySQL/PostgreSQL** view gives you an insight into what your MySQL processes are currently doing:

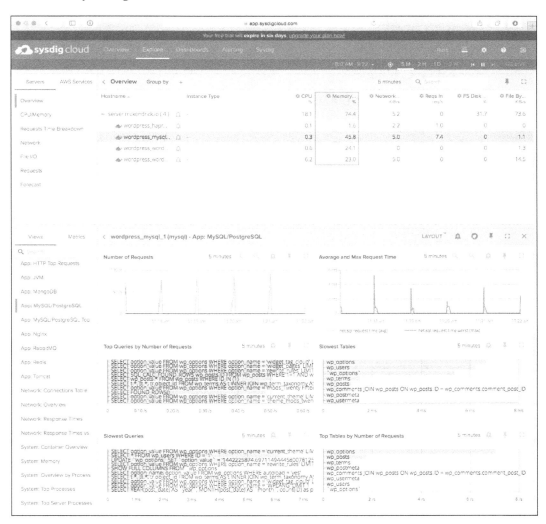

Here, you can see that view in the bottom section has instantly updated to give a wealth of information on what has been happening in the last 5 minutes within MySQL.

Sysdig Cloud supports a number of application views, including:

- Apache
- HAProxy
- NGINX
- RabbitMQ
- Redis
- Tomcat

Each one gives you immediate access to metrics, which even the most experienced SysAdmins will find valuable.

You may have noticed that at the top of the second panel there are also a few icons, these allow you to:

- **Add Alert**: Creates an alert based on the view you have open; it lets you tweak the threshold and also choose how you are notified.
- **Sysdig Capture**: Pressing this brings up a dialog, which lets you record a Sysdig session. Once recorded, the session is transferred to Sysdig Cloud or your own S3 bucket. Once the session is available, you download it or explore it within the web interface.
- **SSH Connect**: Gets a remote shell on the server from the Sysdig Cloud web interface; it is useful if you do not have immediate access to your laptop or desktop machine and you want to do some troubleshooting.
- **Pin to dashboard**: Adds the current view to a custom dashboard.

Out these options icons, the "Add Alert" and "Sysdig Capture" options are probably the ones that you will end up using the most. One final view that I found interesting, is the topology one. It gives you a bird's eye view of your host and containers, this is useful too see the interaction between containers and hosts:

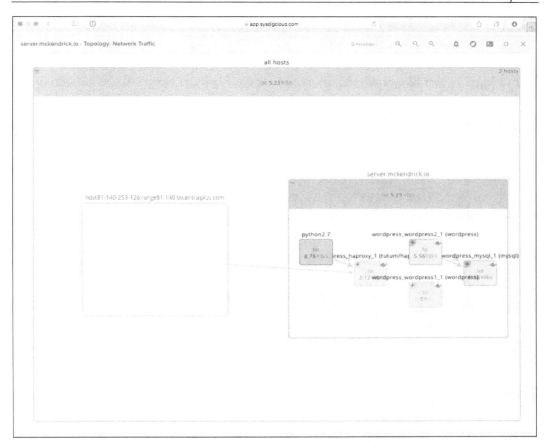

Here, you can see me request a page from the WordPress site (it's in the box on the left), this request hits my host machine (the box on the right). Once it's on the host machine, it is routed to the HAProxy container, which then passes the page request to the Wordpress2 container. From here, the Wordpress2 container interacts with the database that is running on the MySQL container.

Summary and further reading

Although Sysdig Cloud is quite a new service, it feels instantly familiar and fully featured as it is built on top of an already established and respected open source technology. If you like, the level of detail you get from the open source version of Sysdig, then Sysdig Cloud is a natural progression for you to start storing your metrics offsite and also to configure alerts. Some good starting points for learning more about Sysdig Cloud are:

- Video Introduction: https://www.youtube.com/watch?v=p8UVbpw8n24

- Sysdig Cloud Best Practices: http://support.sysdigcloud.com/hc/en-us/articles/204872795-Best-Practices

- Dashboards: http://support.sysdigcloud.com/hc/en-us/articles/204863385-Dashboards

- Sysdig blog: https://sysdig.com/blog/

> If you have launched a cloud instance and are no longer using it, now would be a good time to power the instance down or terminate it altogether. This will ensure that you do not get billed for services that you are not using.

Datadog

Datadog is a full monitoring platform; it supports various servers, platforms, and applications. Wikipedia describes the service as:

"Datadog is a SaaS-based monitoring and analytics platform for IT infrastructure, operations and development teams. It brings together data from servers, databases, applications, tools and services to present a unified view of the applications that run at scale in the cloud."

It uses an agent that is installed on your host machine; this agent sends metrics back to the Datadog service periodically. It also support multiple cloud platforms, such as Amazon Web Services, Microsoft Azure, and OpenStack to name a few.

The aim is to bring all of your servers, applications, and host provider metrics into a single pane of glass; from here, you can create custom dashboards and alerts so that you can be notified of any problem at any level within your infrastructure.

You can sign up for a free trial of the full service at `https://app.datadoghq.com/signup`. You will need at least a trial account to configure the altering, and if your trial has already expired the lite account will do. For more detail on Datadog's pricing structure, please see `https://www.datadoghq.com/pricing/`.

Installing the agent

The agent can be installed either directly on the host machine or as a container. To install directly on the host machine, run the following command and make sure that you use your own unique `DD_API_KEY`:

```
DD_API_KEY=wn5AYlhjRhgn3shcjW14y3yOT09WsF7d bash -c "$(curl -L https://
raw.githubusercontent.com/DataDog/dd-agent/master/packaging/datadog-
agent/source/install_agent.sh)"
```

To run the agent as a container, use the following command and again make sure that you use your own `DD_API_KEY`:

```
sudo docker run -d --name dd-agent -h `hostname` -v /var/run/docker.
sock:/var/run/docker.sock -v /proc/mounts:/host/proc/mounts:ro -v /sys/
fs/cgroup/:/host/sys/fs/cgroup:ro -e API_KEY=wn5AYlhjRhgn3shcjW14y3yOT09W
sF7d datadog/docker-dd-agent
```

Once the agent has been installed, it will call back to Datadog and the host will appear in your account.

If the agent has been installed directly on the host machine then we will need to enable the Docker integration, if you installed the agent using the container then this will have been done for you automatically.

To do this, you first need to allow the Datadog agent access to your Docker installation by adding the `dd-agent` user to the Docker group by running the following command:

```
usermod -a -G docker dd-agent
```

The next step is to create the `docker.yaml` configuration file, luckily the Datadog agent ships with an example configuration file that we can use; copy this in place and then restart the agent:

```
cp -pr /etc/dd-agent/conf.d/docker.yaml.example /etc/dd-agent/conf.d/
docker.yaml
```

```
sudo /etc/init.d/datadog-agent restart
```

Now the agent on our host machine has been configured and the final step is to enable the integration through the website. To do this, go to `https://app.datadoghq.com/` and click on **Integrations**, scroll down and then click on install on **Docker**:

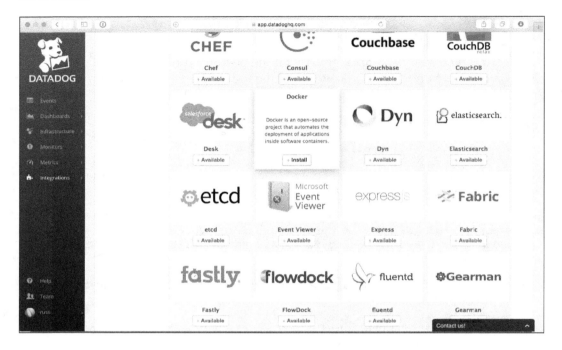

Once you click install, you will be presented with an overview of the integration, click on the **Configuration** tab, this gives instructions on how to configure the agent; as we have already done this step, you can click on **Install Integration**.

You can find more information on installing the agent and the integrations at the following URLs:

- `https://app.datadoghq.com/account/settings#agent`
- `https://app.datadoghq.com/account/settings#integrations`

Exploring the web interface

Now, you have installed the agent and enabled the Docker integration, you can start to have a look around the web interface. To find your host, click on "Infrastructure" in the left-hand side menu.

You should be taken to a screen that contains a map of your infrastructure. Like me, you probably only have a single host machine listed, click on it and some basic stats should appear at the bottom of the screen:

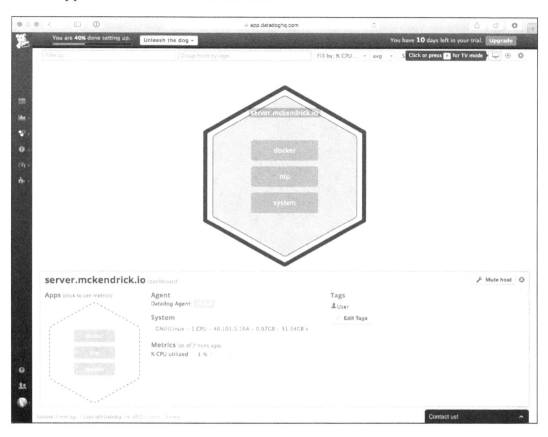

If you don't already have the containers launched, now would be a good time to do so, lets launch the WordPress installation again using:

```
sudo su -
```

```
mkdir ~/wordpress
```

```
curl -L https://raw.githubusercontent.com/russmckendrick/monitoring-
docker/master/chapter05/wordpress/docker-compose.yml > ~/wordpress/
docker-compose.yml
```

```
cd ~/wordpress
```

```
docker-compose up -d
```

Now, go back to the web interface, from there you can click on any of the services listed on the hexagon. This will bring up some basic metrics for the service you have selected. If you click on **docker**, you will see a link for a Docker Dashboard among the various graphs and so on; clicking this will take you to a more detailed view of your containers:

As you can see, this gives us our now familiar break down of the CPU and memory metrics, along with in the top right of the dashboard a breakdown of the container activity on the host machine; this logs events, such as stopping and starting containers.

Datadog currently records the following metrics:

- `docker.containers.running`
- `docker.containers.stopped`

- `docker.cpu.system`
- `docker.cpu.user`
- `docker.images.available`
- `docker.images.intermediate`
- `docker.mem.cache`
- `docker.mem.rss`
- `docker.mem.swap`

From the **Metrics** explorer option in the left-hand side menu, you can start to graph these metrics and once you have the graphs, you can then start to add them to your own custom dashboards or even annotate them. When you annotate a graph, a snapshot is created and the graph shows up in the events queue along with the other events, that have been recorded, such as container stopping and starting:

Also, within the web interface you can configure monitors; these allow you to define triggers, which alert you if your conditions are not met. Alerts can be sent as e-mails or via third party services, such as Slack, Campfire, or PagerDuty.

Summary and further reading

While Datadog's Docker integration only gives you the basic metrics on your containers, it does have a wealth of features and integration with other applications and third parties. If you need to monitor a number of different services alongside your Docker containers, then this service could be for you:

- Home page: `https://www.datadoghq.com`
- Overview: `https://www.datadoghq.com/product/`
- Monitoring Docker with Datadog: `https://www.datadoghq.com/blog/monitor-docker-datadog/`
- Twitter: `https://twitter.com/datadoghq`

> **Please Remember**
>
> If you have launched a cloud instance and are no longer using it then now would be a good time to power the instance down or terminate it altogether. This will ensure that you do not get billed for any services you are not using.

New Relic

New Relic could be considered the granddaddy of SaaS monitoring tools, chances are that if you are a developer you will have heard of New Relic. It has been around for a while and it is the standard to which other SaaS tools compare themselves.

New Relic has grown into several products over the year, currently, they offer:

- **New Relic APM**: The main application performance-monitoring tool. This is what most people will know New Relic for; this toll gives you the code level visibility of your application.
- **New Relic Mobile**: A set of libraries to embed into your native mobile apps, giving APM levels of detail for your iOS and android application.
- **New Relic Insights**: A high-level view of all of the metrics collected by other New Relic services.

- **New Relic Servers**: Monitors your host servers, recording metrics around CPU, RAM, and storage utilization.

- **New Relic Browser**: Gives you an insight into what happens with your web-based applications once they leave your servers and enter your end user's browser

- **New Relic Synthetics**: Monitors your applications responsiveness from various locations around the world.

Rather than looking at all of these offerings that give us an insight into what is happening with our Docker-based code, as that's probably a whole book on its own, we are going to take a look at the server product.

The server monitoring service offered by New Relic is available free of charge, you just need an active New Relic account, you can sign up for an account at `https://newrelic.com/signup/` details on New Relics pricing can be found at their homepage at `http://newrelic.com/`.

Installing the agent

Like the other SaaS offerings we have looked at in this chapter, New Relic Servers has a host-based client, which needs to be able to access the Docker binary. To install this on a CentOS machine, run the following:

```
yum install http://download.newrelic.com/pub/newrelic/el5/i386/newrelic-repo-5-3.noarch.rpm
yum install newrelic-sysmond
```

For Ubuntu, run the following command:

```
echo 'deb http://apt.newrelic.com/debian/ newrelic non-free' | sudo tee /etc/apt/sources.list.d/newrelic.list
wget -O- https://download.newrelic.com/548C16BF.gpg | sudo apt-key add -
apt-get update
apt-get install newrelic-sysmond
```

Now that you have the agent installed, you need to configure the agent with your license key. You can do this with the following command and make sure that you add your license, which can be found in your settings page:

```
nrsysmond-config --set license_key= wn5AYlhjRhgn3shcjW14y3yOT09WsF7d
```

Now that the agent is configured, we need to add the `newrelic` user to the `docker` group so that the agent has access to our container information:

```
usermod -a -G docker newrelic
```

Finally, we need to start the New Relic Server agent and restart Docker:

```
/etc/init.d/newrelic-sysmond restart
```

```
/etc/init.d/docker restart
```

 Restarting Docker will stop the running containers that you have; make sure that you make a note of these using `docker ps` and then start them manually and back up once the Docker service restarts.

You should see your server appear on your New Relic control panel after a few minutes.

Exploring the web interface

Once you have the New Relic server agent installed, configured, and running on your host machine, you will see something similar to the following screenshot when clicking on **Servers** in the top menu:

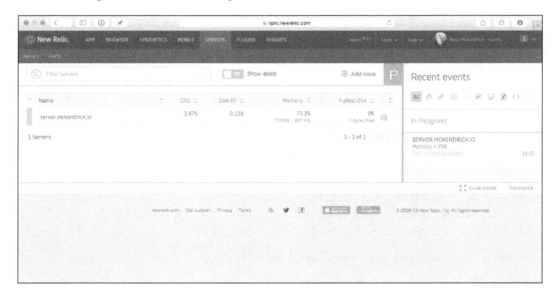

Selecting the server will allow you to start exploring the various metrics that the agent is recording:

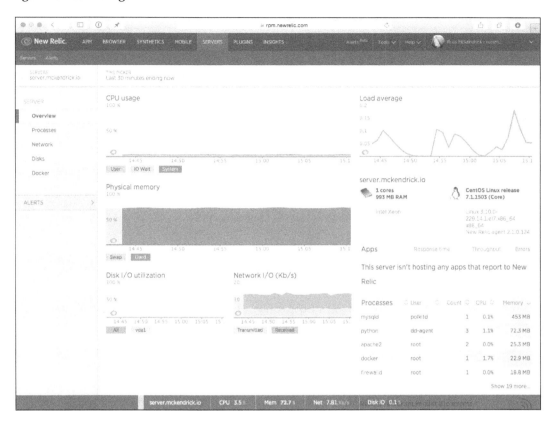

From here, you have the option to drill down further:

- **Overview**: Gives a quick overview of your host machine
- **Processes**: Lists all of the processes that are running both on the host machine and within your containers
- **Network**: Lets you see the network activity for your host machine
- **Disks**: Gives you details on how much space you are using
- **Docker**: Shows you the CPU and memory utilization for your containers

As you may have guessed, we are going to be looking at the **Docker** item next, click on it and you will see a list of your active images:

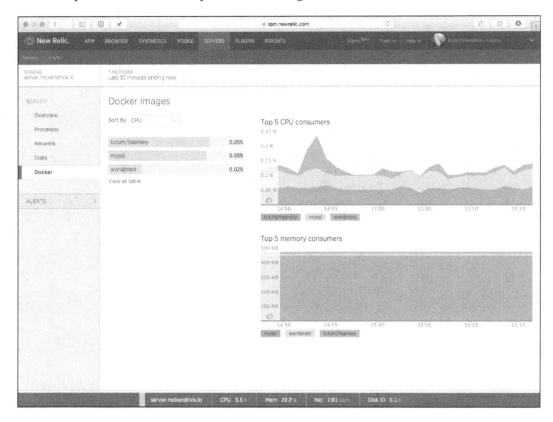

You may have noticed a difference between New Relic and the other services, as you can see New Relic does not show you the running containers, instead it shows you the utilization by Docker image.

In the preceding screenshot, I have four containers active and running the WordPress installation we have used elsewhere in the book. If I wanted a breakdown per container, then I would be out of luck, as demonstrated by the following screen:

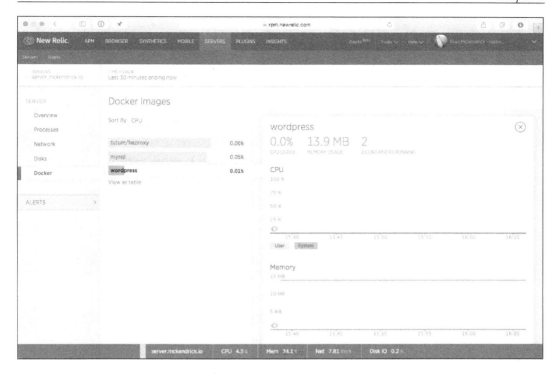

It's a pretty dull screen, but it gives you an idea about what you will see if you are running multiple containers that have been launched using the same image. So how is this useful? Well, coupled with the other services offered by New Relic, it can give you an indication of what your containers were up to when a problem occurred within your application. If you remember the Pets versus Cattle versus Chickens analogy from *Chapter 1*, *Introduction to Docker Monitoring*, we don't necessarily care which container did what; we just want to see the impact it had during the issue we are looking into.

Summary and further reading

Due to the amount of products it offers, New Relic can be a little daunting at first, but if you work with a development team that actively uses New Relic within their day-to-day workflow, then having all of the information about your infrastructure alongside this data can be both valuable and necessary, especially during an issue:

- New Relic Server monitoring: `http://newrelic.com/server-monitoring`

- New Relic and Docker: `http://newrelic.com/docker/`

- Twitter: `https://twitter.com/NewRelic`

If you have launched a cloud instance and are no longer using it then, now is a good time to power the instance down or terminate it altogether, this will ensure you do not get billed for any services you are not using.

Summary

Which SaaS service you choose depends on your circumstances, there are a number of questions you should ask yourself before you start evaluating the SaaS offerings:

- How many containers would you like to monitor?
- How many host machines do you have?
- Is there a non-containerized infrastructure you need to monitor?
- What metrics do you need from the monitoring service?
- How long should the data be retained for?
- Could other departments, such as development and utilize the service?

We covered just three of the available SaaS options in this chapter, there are other options available, such as:

- Ruxit: https://ruxit.com/docker-monitoring/
- Scout: https://scoutapp.com/plugin_urls/19761-docker-monitor
- Logentries: https://logentries.com/insights/server-monitoring/
- Sematext: http://sematext.com/spm/integrations/docker-monitoring.html

Monitoring servers and services are only as good as the metrics you collect, if possible and if your budget allows, you should take full advantage of the services offered by your chosen providers, as more data being recorded by a single provider will only benefit you when it comes to analyzing problems with not only your containerized applications, but also with your infrastructure, code and even your cloud provider.

For example, if you are monitoring your host machine using the same service as you use to monitor your containers, then by using the custom graphing functions, you should be able to create overlay graphs of CPU load spikes of both your host machine and your container. This is a lot more useful than trying to compare two different graphs from different systems side by side.

In the next chapter, we will look at an often-overlooked part of monitoring: shipping your log files away from your containers/hosts to a single location so that they can be monitored and reviewed.

7
Collecting Application Logs from within the Container

One of the most overlooked parts of monitoring are log files generated by the application or services such as NGINX, MySQL, Apache, and so on. So far we have looked at various ways of recording the CPU and RAM utilization of the processes within your containers are at a point in time, now its time to do the same for the log files.

If you are running your containers as Cattle or Chickens, then the way you deal with the issues to destroy and relaunch your container either manually or automatically is important. While this should fix the immediate problem, it does not help with tracking down the root cause of the issue and if you don't know that then how can you attempt to resolve it so that it does not reoccur.

In this chapter, we will look at how we can get the content of the log files for the applications running within our containers to the central location so that they are available, even if you have to destroy and replace a container. We are going to cover the following topics in this chapter:

- How to view container logs?
- Deploying an "ELK" stack using a Docker containers stack to ship the logs to
- Reviewing your logs
- What third party options are available?

Viewing container logs

Like the `docker top` command, there is a very basic way of viewing logs. When you use the `docker logs` command, you are actually viewing the STDOUT and STDERR of the processes that are running within the container.

 For more information on Standard Streams, please see
https://en.wikipedia.org/wiki/Standard_streams.

As you can see from the following screenshot, the simplest thing you have to do is run `docker logs` followed by your container name:

```
vagrant@docker:/monitoring_docker/chapter05/wordpress — ssh • vagrant ssh — 181×36
[vagrant@docker ~]$ cd /monitoring_docker/chapter05/wordpress/
[vagrant@docker wordpress]$ docker-compose up -d
Creating wordpress_mysql_1...
Creating wordpress_wordpress1_1...
Creating wordpress_wordpress2_1...
Creating wordpress_haproxy_1...
[vagrant@docker wordpress]$ docker-compose ps
        Name                    Command              State              Ports
------------------------------------------------------------------------------------------------
wordpress_haproxy_1      python /haproxy/main.py      Up      1936/tcp, 443/tcp, 0.0.0.0:80->80/tcp
wordpress_mysql_1        /entrypoint.sh mysqld        Up      3306/tcp
wordpress_wordpress1_1   /entrypoint.sh apache2-for   Up      80/tcp
wordpress_wordpress2_1   /entrypoint.sh apache2-for   Up      80/tcp
[vagrant@docker wordpress]$ docker logs wordpress_wordpress1_1
WordPress not found in /var/www/html - copying now...
WARNING: /var/www/html is not empty - press Ctrl+C now if this is an error!
+ ls -A
index.html
+ sleep 10
Complete! WordPress has been successfully copied to /var/www/html
AH00558: apache2: Could not reliably determine the server's fully qualified domain name, using 172.17.0.6. Set the 'ServerName' directive globally to suppress this message
AH00558: apache2: Could not reliably determine the server's fully qualified domain name, using 172.17.0.6. Set the 'ServerName' directive globally to suppress this message
[Sat Oct 10 10:13:54.201615 2015] [mpm_prefork:notice] [pid 1] AH00163: Apache/2.4.10 (Debian) PHP/5.6.14 configured -- resuming normal operations
[Sat Oct 10 10:13:54.201654 2015] [core:notice] [pid 1] AH00094: Command line: 'apache2 -D FOREGROUND'
[vagrant@docker wordpress]$ []
```

To see this on your own host, let's launch the WordPress installation from `chapter05` using the following commands:

```
cd /monitoring_docker/chapter05/wordpress/
docker-compose up -d
docker logs wordpress_wordpress1_1
```

You can extend the `dockerlogs` command by adding the following flags before your container name:

- `-f` or `--follow` will stream the logs in real time
- `-t` or `--timestamps` will show a timestamp at the start of each line
- `--tail="5"` will show the last *x* number of lines
- `--since="5m00s"` will show only the entries for the last 5 minutes

Using the WordPress installation that we have just launched, try running the following commands:

```
docker logs --tail="2" wordpress_wordpress1_1
```

This will show the last two lines of the logs, you can add timestamps using:

```
docker logs --tail="2" -timestamps wordpress_wordpress1_1
```

As you can see in the following terminal output, you can also string commands together to form a very basic query language:

The downside of using `docker logs` is exactly the same as using `docker top`, in that it is only available locally and the logs are only present for the time the container is around, you can view the logs of a stopped container, but once the container is removed, so are the logs.

ELK Stack

Similar to some of the technologies that we have covered in this book, an ELK stack really deserves a book by itself; in fact, there are books for each of the elements that make an ELK stack, these elements are:

- Elasticsearch is a powerful search server, which has been developed with modern workloads in mind
- Logstash sits between your data source and Elasticsearch services; it transforms your data in real time to a format, which Elasticsearch can understand.
- Kibana is in front of your Elasticsearch services and allows you to query your data in a feature-rich web-based dashboard.

There are a lot of moving parts with an ELK stack, so to simplify things, we will use a prebuilt stack for the purpose of testing; however, you probably don't want to use this stack in production.

Starting the stack

Let's launch a fresh vagrant host on which to run the ELK stack:

```
[russ@mac ~]$ cd ~/Documents/Projects/monitoring-docker/vagrant-centos/
[russ@mac ~]$ vagrant up
Bringing machine 'default' up with 'virtualbox' provider...
==> default: Importing base box 'russmckendrick/centos71'...
==> default: Matching MAC address for NAT networking...
==> default: Checking if box 'russmckendrick/centos71' is up to date...


. . . . .


==> default: => Installing docker-engine ...
==> default: => Configuring vagrant user ...
==> default: => Starting docker-engine ...
==> default: => Installing docker-compose ...
==> default: => Finished installation of Docker
[russ@mac ~]$ vagrant ssh
```

Now, we have a clean host that is up and running, we can start the stack by running the following commands:

```
[vagrant@docker ~]$ cd /monitoring_docker/chapter07/elk/
[vagrant@docker elk]$ docker-compose up -d
```

As you may have noticed, it did more that just pull down some images; what happened was:

- An Elasticsearch container was launched using the official image from https://hub.docker.com/_/elasticsearch/.

- A Logstash container was launched using the official image from https://hub.docker.com/_/logstash/, it was also launched with our own configuration, which means that our installation listens for logs sent from Logspout (more about that in a minute).

- A custom Kibana image was built using the official image from
  `https://hub.docker.com/_/kibana/`. All it did was add a small script
  to ensure that Kibana doesn't start until our Elasticsearch container is fully
  up and running. It was then launched with a custom configuration file.

- A custom Logspout container was built using the official image from
  `https://hub.docker.com/r/gliderlabs/logspout/` and then we
  added a custom module so that Logspout could talk to Logstash.

Once `docker-compose` has finished building and launching the stack you should be
able to see the following when running `docker-compose ps`:

```
                    vagrant@docker:/monitoring_docker/chapter07/elk — ssh • vagrant ssh — 122×24
[vagrant@docker elk]$ docker-compose ps
      Name                    Command              State            Ports
--------------------------------------------------------------------------------------------
elk_elasticsearch_1   /docker-entrypoint.sh elas ...   Up      0.0.0.0:9200->9200/tcp, 9300/tcp
elk_kibana_1          /docker-entrypoint.sh /tmp ...   Up      0.0.0.0:8080->5601/tcp
elk_logspout_1        /bin/logspout                    Up      8000/tcp
elk_logstash_1        /docker-entrypoint.sh logs ...   Up      0.0.0.0:5000->5000/tcp
[vagrant@docker elk]$ []
```

We now have our ELK stack up and running, as you may have noticed, there is an
additional container running and giving us an ELK-L stack, so what is Logspout?

Logspout

If we were to launch Elasticsearch, Logstash, and Kibana containers, we should
have a functioning ELK stack but we will have a lot of configuration to do to get
our container logs into Elasticsearch.

Since Docker 1.6, you have been able to configure logging drivers, this meant that it
is possible to launch a container and have it send its STDOUT and STDERR to a Syslog
Server, which will be Logstash in our case; however, this means that you will have to
add something similar to the following options each time we launch a container:

`--log-driver=syslog --log-opt syslog-address=tcp://elk_logstash_1:5000`

This is where Logspout comes in, it has been designed to collect all of the STDOUT and STDERR messages on a host machine by intercepting the messages that are being collected by the Docker process and then it routes them to our Logstash instance in a format that is understood by Elasticsearch.

Just as the log-driver, it supports Syslog out of the box; however, there is a third party module that transforms the output to JSON, which Logstash understands. As a part of our build we downloaded, compiled and configured the module.

You can find out more about Logspout and logging drivers at the following:

- Official Logspout image:
  `https://hub.docker.com/r/gliderlabs/logspout/`

- Logspout Project page: `https://github.com/gliderlabs/logspout`

- Logspout Logstash module:
  `https://github.com/looplab/logspout-logstash`

- Docker 1.6 release notes:
  `https://blog.docker.com/2015/04/docker-release-1-6/`

- Docker Logging Drivers:
  `https://docs.docker.com/reference/logging/overview/`

Reviewing the logs

So now, we have our ELK running and a mechanism in place to stream all of the STDOUT and STDERR messages generated by our containers into Logstash, which in turn routes the data into Elasticsearch. Now its time to view the logs in Kibana. To access Kibana go to `http://192.168.33.10:8080/` in your browser; when you access the page, you will be asked to **Configure an index pattern**, the default index pattern will be fine for our needs so just click the **Create** button.

Once you do, you will see a list of the index patterns, these are taken directly from the Logspout output, and you should notice the following items in the index:

- `docker.name`: The name of container
- `docker.id`: The full container ID
- `docker.image`: The name of the image used to launch the image

From here, if you were to click on **Discover** in the top menu you would see
something similar to the following page:

In the screenshot, you will see that I have recently launched the WordPress stack and
we have been using it throughout the book, using the following commands:

```
[vagrant@docker elk]$ cd /monitoring_docker/chapter05/wordpress/
[vagrant@docker wordpress]$ docker-compose up -d
```

To give you an idea of what is being logged, here is the raw JSON taken from Elasticseach for running the WordPress installation script:

```
{
  "_index": "logstash-2015.10.11",
  "_type": "logs",
  "_id": "AVBW8ewRnBVdqUV1XVOj",
  "_score": null,
  "_source": {
    "message": "172.17.0.11 - - [11/Oct/2015:12:48:26 +0000]
\"POST /wp-admin/install.php?step=1 HTTP/1.1\" 200 2472
\"http://192.168.33.10/wp-admin/install.php\" \"Mozilla/5.0
(Macintosh; Intel Mac OS X 10_11) AppleWebKit/601.1.56 (KHTML, like
Gecko) Version/9.0 Safari/601.1.56\"",
    "docker.name": "/wordpress_wordpress1_1",
    "docker.id":
"0ba42876867f738b9da0b9e3adbb1f0f8044b7385ce9b3a8a3b9ec60d9f5436c",
    "docker.image": "wordpress",
    "docker.hostname": "0ba42876867f",
    "@version": "1",
    "@timestamp": "2015-10-11T12:48:26.641Z",
    "host": "172.17.0.4"
  },
  "fields": {
    "@timestamp": [
      1444567706641
    ]
  },
  "sort": [
    1444567706641
  ]
}
```

From here, you can start to use the free text search box and build up some quite complex queries to drill down into your container's STDOUT and STDERR logs.

What about production?

As mentioned at the top of this section, you probably don't want to run your production ELK stack using the docker-compose file, which accompanies this chapter. First of all, you will want your Elasticsearch data to be stored on a persistent volume and you more than likely want your Logstash service to be highly available.

There are numerous guides on how to configure a highly available ELK stack, as well as, the hosted services from Elastic, which is the creator of Elasticsearch, and also Amazon Web Services, which offers an Elasticsearch service:

- ELK tutorial: `https://www.youtube.com/watch?v=ge8uHdmtb1M`

- Found from Elastic: `https://www.elastic.co/found`

- Amazon Elasticsearch Service:
  `https://aws.amazon.com/elasticsearch-service/`

Looking at third party options

There are a few options when it comes to hosting central logging for your containers external to your own server instances. Some of these are:

- Log Entries: `https://logentries.com/`

- Loggly: `https://www.loggly.com/`

Both of these services offer a free tier. Log Entries also offers a "Logentries DockerFree" account that you can find out more about at `https://logentries.com/docker/`

 As recommended in the *Exploring Third Party Options* chapter, it is best to use a cloud service when evaluating third party services. The remainder of this chapter assumes that you are running a cloud host.

Let's look at configuring the Log Entries on an external server, first of all you need to have signed up for an account at `https://logentries.com/`. Once you have signed up, you should be taken to a page in which your logs will eventually be displayed.

To start, click on the **Add new log** button in the top-right corner of the page and then click the Docker logo in the **Platforms** section.

You have to name your set of logs in the **Select set** section, so give a name to your log set. You now have the choice of building your own container locally using the Docker file from `https://github.com/logentries/docker-logentries`:

```
git clone https://github.com/logentries/docker-logentries.git
cd docker-logentries
docker build -t docker-logentries .
```

After running the preceding command, you will get the following output:

Before you start your container, you will need to generate an access token for your log set by clicking on **Generate Log Token**. Once you have this, you can launch your locally built containers using the following command (replace the token with the one you have just generated):

```
docker run -d -v /var/run/docker.sock:/var/run/docker.sock docker-
logentries -t wn5AYlh-jRhgn3shc-jW14y3yO-TO9WsF7d -j
```

You can download the image straight from the Docker hub by running:

```
docker run -d -v /var/run/docker.sock:/var/run/docker.sock logentries/
docker-logentries -t wn5AYlh-jRhgn3shc-jW14y3yO-TO9WsF7d -j
```

It's worth pointing out that the automatically generated instructions given by Log Entries launches the container in the foreground, rather than detaching from the container once it has been launched like the preceding instructions.

Once you have the `docker-logentries` container up and running, you should start to see logs from your container streamed in real-time to your dashboard:

From here, you will be able to query your logs, create dashboards, and create alerts depending on the account option you go for.

Summary

In this chapter, we have covered how to query the STDOUT and STDERR output from your containers using the tool built into Docker, how to ship the messages to an external source, our ELK stack, and how to store the messages even after the container has been terminated. Finally, we have looked at a few of the third-party services who offer services to which you can stream your logs.

So why go to all of this effort? Monitoring isn't just about keeping and querying CPU, RAM, HDD, and Network utilization metrics; there is no point in knowing if there was a CPU spike an hour ago if you don't have access to the log files to see if any errors were being generated at that time.

The services we have covered in this chapter offer the quickest and most efficient insights into what can quickly become a complex dataset.

In the next chapter, we will look at all of the services and concepts we have covered in the book and apply them to some real world scenarios.

What Are the Next Steps?

8

In this final chapter, we will look at the next steps you can take to monitor your containers, by talking about the benefits of adding alerts to your monitoring. Also, we will cover some different scenarios and also which type of monitoring is appropriate for each of them:

- Common problems (performance, availability, and so on) and which type of monitoring is best for your situation.

- What are the benefits of alerting on the metrics you are collecting and what are the options?

Some scenarios

To look at which type of monitoring you might want to implement for your container-based applications, we should work through a few different example configurations that your container-based applications could be deploying into. First, let's remind ourselves about Pets, Cattle, Chickens, and Snowflakes.

Pets, Cattle, Chickens, and Snowflakes

Back in the *Chapter 1, Introduction to Docker Monitoring*, we spoke about Pets, Cattle, Chickens, and Snowflakes; in that chapter, we described what each term meant when it was applied to modern cloud deployments. Here, we will go into a little more detail about how the terms can be applied to your containers.

Pets

For your containers to be considered a Pet, you will be more than likely to be running either a single or a small number of fixed containers on a designated host.

Each one of these containers could be considered a single point of failure; if any one of them goes down, it will more than likely result in errors for your application. Worst still, if the host machine goes down for any reason, your entire application will be offline.

This is a typical deployment method for most of our first steps with Docker, and in no way should it be considered bad, frowned upon, or not recommend; as long as you are aware of the limitations, you will be fine.

This pattern can also be used to describe most development environments, as you are constantly reviewing its health and tuning as needed.

You will more than likely be hosting the machine on your local computer or on a hosting service such as DigitalOcean (`https://www.digitalocean.com/`).

Cattle

For the bulk of production or business critical deployments, you should aim to launch your containers in a configuration that allows them to automatically recover themselves after a failure, or, when more capacity is needed, additional containers are launched and then terminated when the scaling event is over.

You will more than likely be using a public cloud-based service as follows:

- Amazon EC2 Container Service: `https://aws.amazon.com/ecs/`
- Google Container Engine: `https://cloud.google.com/container-engine/`
- Joyent Triton: `https://www.joyent.com/blog/understanding-triton-containers/`

Alternatively, you will be hosting on your own servers using a Docker-friendly and cluster-aware operating system as follows:

- CoreOS: `https://coreos.com/`
- RancherOS: `http://rancher.com/rancher-os/`

You won't care so much as to where a container is launched within your cluster of hosts, as long as you can route traffic to it. To add more capacity to the cluster, you will be bringing up additional hosts when needed and removing them from the cluster when not needed in order to save on costs.

Chickens

Its more than likely you will be using containers to launch, process data, and then terminate. This can happen anytime from once a day to several times a minute. You will be using a distributed scheduler as follows:

- Kubernetes by Google: http://kubernetes.io/
- Apache Mesos: http://mesos.apache.org/

Because of this, you will have a large number of containers launching and terminating within your cluster; you definitely won't care about where a container is launched or even how traffic is routed to it, as long as your data is processed correctly and passed back to your application.

Like the cluster described in the *Cattle* section's description, hosts will be added and removed automatically, probably in response to scheduled peaks such as end of month reporting or seasonal sales and so on.

Snowflakes

I hope one of the things you took away from the first chapter is that if you have any servers or services that you consider being Snowflakes, then you should do something to retire them as soon as possible.

Luckily, due to the way the containerizing of your applications works, you should never be able to create a snowflake using Docker, as your containerized environment should always be reproducible, either because you have the Docker file (everyone makes backups right?) or you have a working copy of the container image because you have exported the container as a whole using the built-in tools.

 Sometimes it may not be possible to create a container using a Docker file. Instead, you can backup or migrate your containers by using the export command. For more information on exporting your containers, see the following URL:

https://docs.docker.com/reference/commandline/export/

If you find yourself in this position, let me be the first to congratulate you on mitigating a future disaster by promoting your Snowflake into a Pet or even Cattle ahead of any problems.

Still running a Snowflake?

If you find yourself still running a Snowflake server or service, I cannot stress enough that you look at documenting, migrating, or updating the Snowflake as soon as possible. There is no point in monitoring a service that may be impossible for you to recover. Remember that there are containers for old technologies, such as PHP4, if you really need to run them.

Scenario one

You are running a personal WordPress website using the official containers from the Docker Hub; the containers have been launched using a Docker Compose file like the one we have used several times throughout this book.

You have the Docker Compose file stored in a GitHub repository and you can take snapshots of the host machine as a backup. As it's your own blog, you are fine running it on a single cloud-based host.

A suitable monitoring will be as follows:

- Docker stats
- Docker top
- Docker logs
- cAdvisor
- Sysdig

As you are running a single host machine that you are treating as a backup, there is no real need for you to ship your log files to a central location as odds are your host machines; like the containers, its hosting will be online for months or possibly even years.

It is unlikely that you will need to dig too deeply into your containers' historical performance stats, as most of the tuning and troubleshooting will be done in real time as problems occur.

With the monitoring tools suggested, you will be able to get a good insight into what is happening within your containers in real time, and to get more than enough information on processes that are consuming too much RAM and CPU, along with any error messages from within the containers.

You may want to enable a service such as Pingdom (`https://www.pingdom.com/`) or Uptime Robot (`http://uptimerobot.com/`). These services poll your website every few minutes to ensure that the URL you configure them to, check whether its loading within a certain time or at all. If they detect any slowdown or failures with the page loading, they can be configured to send an initial alert to notify you that there is a potential issue, such as both the services mentioned have a free tier.

Scenario two

You are running a custom e-commerce application that needs to be highly available and also scale during your peak times. You are using a public cloud service and the toolset that comes with it to launch containers and route traffic to them.

A suitable monitoring will be as follows:

- cAdvisor + Prometheus
- Zabbix
- Sysdig Cloud
- New Relic Server Monitoring
- Datadog
- ELK + Logspout
- Log Entries
- Loggly

With this scenario, there is a business need to not only be notified about container and host failures, but also to hold your monitoring data and logs away from your host servers so that you can properly review historical information. You may also need to keep logs for PCI compliance or internal auditing for a fixed period of time.

Depending on your budget, you can achieve this by hosting your own monitoring (Zabbix and Prometheus) and central logging (ELK) stacks somewhere within your infrastructure.

You can also choose to run a few different third-party tools such as combining tools that monitor performance, for example, Sysdig Cloud or Datadog, with a central logging service, such as Log Entries or Loggly.

If appropriate, you can also run a combination of self-hosted and third-party tools.

While the self-hosted option may appear to be the most budget-friendly option, there are some considerations to take into account, as follows:

- Your monitoring needs to be hosted away from your application. There is no point in having your monitoring installed on the same host as your application; what will alert you if the host fails?

- Your monitoring needs to be highly available; do you have the infrastructure to do this? If your application needs to be highly available, then so does your monitoring.

- You need to have enough capacity. Do you have the capacity to be able to store log files and metrics going back a month, 6 months, or a year?

If you are going to have to invest in any of the preceding options, then it will be worth weighing up the costs of investing in both the infrastructure and the management of your own monitoring solution against using a third-party that will offer the preceding options as a service.

If you are using a container-only operating system such as CoreOS or RancherOS, then you will need to choose a service whose agent or collector can be executed from within a container, as you will not be able to install the agent binaries directly on the OS.

You will also need to ensure that your host machine is configured to start the agents/collectors on boot. This will ensure that as soon as the host machine joins a cluster (which is typically when containers will start to popup on the host), it is already sending metrics to your chosen monitoring services.

Scenario three

Your application launches a container each time your API is called from your frontend application; the container takes the user input from a database, processes it, and then passes the results back to your front end application. Once the data has been successfully processed, the container is terminated. You are using a distributed scheduling system to launch the containers.

A suitable monitoring will be as follows:

- Zabbix
- Sysdig Cloud
- Datadog
- ELK + Logspout
- Log Entries
- Loggly

In this scenario, you more than likely do not want to monitor things such as CPU and RAM utilization. These containers after all should only be around for a few minutes, and also your scheduler will launch the container on the host machine where there is enough capacity for the task to execute.

Instead, you will probably want to keep a record to verify that the container launched and terminated as expected. You will also want to make sure that you log the STDOUT and STDERR from the container while it is active, as once the container has been terminated, it will be impossible for you to get these messages back.

With the tools listed in the preceding points, you should be able to build some quite useful queries to get a detailed insight into how your short run processes are performing.

For example, you will be able to get the average lifetime of a container, as you know the time the container was launched and when it was terminated; knowing this will then allow you to set a trigger to alert you if any containers are around for any longer than you would expect them to be.

A little more about alerting

A lot of the tools we have looked at in this book offer at least some sort of basic alerting functionality; the million-dollar question is should you enable it?

A lot of this is dependent on the type of application you are running and how the containers have been deployed. As we have already mentioned a few times in this chapter, you should never really have a Snowflake container; this leaves us with Pets, Cattle, and Chickens.

Chickens

As already discussed in the previous section, you probably don't need to worry about getting alerts for RAM, CPU, and hard drive performance on a cluster that is configured to run Chickens.

Your containers should not be up long enough to experience any real problems; however, should there be any unexpected spikes, your scheduler will probably have enough intelligence to distribute your containers to hosts that have the most available resources at that time.

You will need to know if any of your containers have been running longer than you expect them to be up; for example, a process in a container that normally takes no more than 60 seconds is still running after 5 minutes.

This not only means that there is a potential problem, it also means that you find yourself running hosts that only contain stale containers.

Cattle and Pets

When it comes to setting up alerts on Cattle or Pets, you have a few options.

You will more than likely want to receive alerts based on CPU and RAM utilization for both the host machine and the containers, as this could indicate a potential problem that could cause slow down within the application and also loss of business.

As mentioned previously, you will probably also want to be alerted if your application starts to serve the content that is unexpected. For example, a host and a container will quite happily sit there serving an application error.

You can use a service such as Pingdom, Zabbix, or New Relic to load a page and check for the content in the footer; if this content is missing, then an alert can be sent.

Depending on how fluid your infrastructure is, in a Cattle configuration, you will probably want to be alerted when containers spin up and down, as this will indicate periods of high traffic/transactions.

Sending alerts

Sending alerts differs for each tool, for example, an alert could be as simple as sending an email to inform you that there is an issue to the sounding of an audible alert in a **Network Operations Center** (**NOC**) when the CPU load of a container goes above five, or the load on the host goes above 10.

For those of you who require an on-call team to be alerted, most of the software we have covered has some level of integration alert aggregation services such as PagerDuty (`https://www.pagerduty.com`).

These aggregation services either intercept your alert emails or allow services to make API calls to them. When triggered, they can be configured to place phone calls, send SMS messages, and even escalate to secondary on-call technician if an alert has not been flagged down within a definable time.

I can't think of any cases where you shouldn't look at enabling alerting, after all, it's always best to know about anything that could effect your application before your end users do.

How much alerting you enable is really down to what you are using your containers for; however, I would recommend that you review all your alerts regularly and also actively tune your configuration.

The last thing you want is a configuration that produces too many false positives or one that is too twitchy, as you do not want the team who receives your alerts to become desensitized to the alerts that you are generating.

For example, if a critical CPU alert is triggered every 30 minutes because of a scheduled job, then you will probably need to review the sensitivity of the alert, otherwise it is easy for the engineer to simply dismiss a critical alert without thinking about it, as "this alert comes every half an hour and will be ok in a few minutes", when your entire application could be unresponsive.

Keeping up

While Docker has been built on top of well-established technologies such as **Linux Containers (LXC)**, these have traditionally been difficult to configure and manage, especially for non-system administrators.

Docker removes almost all the barriers to entry, allowing everyone with a small amount of command-line experience to launch and manage their own container-based applications.

This has forced a lot of the supporting tools to also lower their barrier to entry. Software that once required careful planning to deploy, such as some of the monitoring tools we covered in this book, can now be deployed and configured in minutes rather than hours.

Docker is also a very fast-moving technology; while it has been considered production-ready for a while, new features are being added and existing features are improved with regular updates.

So far, in 2015, there have been 11 releases of Docker Engine; of these, only six have been minor updates that fix bugs, and the rest have all been major updates. Details of each release can be found in the project's Changelog, which can be found at `https://github.com/docker/docker/blob/master/CHANGELOG.md`.

Because of the pace of development of Docker, it is import that you also update any monitoring tools you deploy. This is not only to keep up with new features, but also to ensure that you don't loose any functionality due to changes in the way in which Docker works.

This attitude of updating monitoring clients/tools can be a bit of a change for some administrators who maybe in the past would have configured a monitoring agent on a server and then not thought about it again.

Summary

As discussed in this chapter, Docker is a fast moving technology. While this book has been in production, there have been three major versions released from 1.7 to 1.9; with each release Docker has become more stable and more powerful.

In this chapter, we have looked at different ways to implement the technologies that have been discussed in the previous chapters of this book. By now, you should have an idea of which approach is appropriate to monitor your containers and host machines, for both your application and for the way the application has been deployed using Docker.

No matter which approach you chose to take, it is important that you stay up-to-date with Docker's development and also the new monitoring technologies as they emerge, the following links are good starting points to keep yourself informed:

- Docker Engineering Blog:
  `http://blog.docker.com/category/engineering/`
- Docker on Twitter: `https://twitter.com/docker`
- Docker on Reddit: `https://www.reddit.com/r/docker`
- Docker on Stack Overflow:
  `http://stackoverflow.com/questions/tagged/docker`

One of the reasons why the Docker project has been embraced by developers, system administrators and even enterprise companies is because it is able to move at a quick pace, while adding more features and very impressively maintaining its ease of use and flexibility.

Over the next 12 months, the technology is set to be even more widespread; the importance of ensuring that you are capturing useful performance metrics and logs from your containers will become more critical and I hope that this book has helped you start your journey into monitoring Docker.

Index

Symbol

--privileged flag
about 27
URL 27

A

alerts
enabling 117
sending 119
setting up, on Cattle 118
setting up, on Chickens 118
setting up, on Pets 118
Amazon EC2 Container Service
URL 112
Amazon Web Services
URL 73
Apache Mesos
URL 113
Atomic
URL 76

B

backslash
using 27

C

cAdvisor
about 25, 26
compiling, from source 28, 29
executing, container used 26, 27
reference link 44

Cattle
about 3
alerts, setting up 118
containers, deploying onto 112
Changelog, Docker
URL 120
Chickens
about 3
alerts, setting up 118
containers, deploying onto 113
cloud
Docker, deploying in 74, 75
Cloudscaling
reference link 3
container
used, for executing cAdvisor 26, 27
Container Down 60
container logs
viewing 100, 101
containers
comparing, to host machine 59
deploying, onto Cattle 112
deploying, onto Chickens 113
deploying, onto Pets 112
deploying, onto Snowflakes 113, 114
resource utilization, tracking 20
containers, monitoring
scenarios 114-117
container stats
driver status 36
images 37
subcontainers 36
viewing 36
CoreOS
URL 76

Thank you for buying
Monitoring Docker

About Packt Publishing

Packt, pronounced 'packed', published its first book, *Mastering phpMyAdmin for Effective MySQL Management*, in April 2004, and subsequently continued to specialize in publishing highly focused books on specific technologies and solutions.

Our books and publications share the experiences of your fellow IT professionals in adapting and customizing today's systems, applications, and frameworks. Our solution-based books give you the knowledge and power to customize the software and technologies you're using to get the job done. Packt books are more specific and less general than the IT books you have seen in the past. Our unique business model allows us to bring you more focused information, giving you more of what you need to know, and less of what you don't.

Packt is a modern yet unique publishing company that focuses on producing quality, cutting-edge books for communities of developers, administrators, and newbies alike. For more information, please visit our website at www.packtpub.com.

About Packt Open Source

In 2010, Packt launched two new brands, Packt Open Source and Packt Enterprise, in order to continue its focus on specialization. This book is part of the Packt Open Source brand, home to books published on software built around open source licenses, and offering information to anybody from advanced developers to budding web designers. The Open Source brand also runs Packt's Open Source Royalty Scheme, by which Packt gives a royalty to each open source project about whose software a book is sold.

Writing for Packt

We welcome all inquiries from people who are interested in authoring. Book proposals should be sent to author@packtpub.com. If your book idea is still at an early stage and you would like to discuss it first before writing a formal book proposal, then please contact us; one of our commissioning editors will get in touch with you.

We're not just looking for published authors; if you have strong technical skills but no writing experience, our experienced editors can help you develop a writing career, or simply get some additional reward for your expertise.

Learning Docker

ISBN: 978-1-78439-7937   Paperback: 240 pages

Optimize the power of Docker to run your applications quickly and easily

1. Learn to compose, use, and publish the Docker containers.

2. Leverage the features of Docker to deploy your existing applications.

3. Explore real world examples of securing and managing Docker containers.

Docker Cookbook

ISBN: 978-1-78398-486-2   Paperback: 248 pages

80 hands-on recipes to efficiently work with the Docker 1.6 environment on Linux

1. Provides practical techniques and knowledge of various emerging and developing APIs to help you create scalable services.

2. Create, manage, and automate production-quality services while dealing with inherent issues.

3. Each recipe is carefully organized with instructions to complete the task efficiently.

Please check **www.PacktPub.com** for information on our titles

Docker for Web Developers [Video]

ISBN: 978-1-78439-067-9   Duration: 01:31 hours

Accelerate your web development skills on real web projects in record time with Docker

1. Supercharge your web development process while ensuring that everything works smoothly.

2. Win at 2048 using Docker's commit and restore functionality.

3. Use the Docker Hub workflow to automate the rebuilding of your web projects.

Orchestrating Docker

ISBN: 978-1-78398-478-7   Paperback: 154 pages

Manage and deploy Docker services to containerize applications efficiently

1. Set up your own Heroku-like PaaS by getting accustomed to the Docker ecosystem.

2. Run your applications on development machines, private servers, or the cloud, with minimal cost of a virtual machine.

3. A comprehensive guide to the smooth management and development of Docker containers and its services.

Please check **www.PacktPub.com** for information on our titles